Igniting Your Writing!

Igniting Your Writing!

Sandy Larsen

Merritt Park Press
Greenville, Illinois

**For all young writers
and those who encourage them**

© 2002 Sandy Larsen

All rights reserved. Except as stated, no part of this book may be reproduced in any form without written permission from Merritt Park Press.

The images used herein were obtained from IMSI's MasterClips Collection, 1895 Francisco Blvd. East, San Rafael, CA 94901-5506, USA.

ISBN 0-9666677-4-3

Library of Congress Control Number 2002199733

Merritt Park Press
910 N. Elm St.
Greenville, IL 62246
dslarsen@merrittpark.com
618-664-2207

www.merrittpark.com

www.homeschoolwriting.com

Contents

How to Use *Igniting Your Writing!* 6

A. Word Play
1. Word Trade 8
2. Sentence Stretch 10
3. Sentence Shrink 12
4. Flip It! (Word Order) 14

B. Parts of Speech: Part of Writing
1. Action! (Verbs) 16
2. What *Is* This? (Nouns) 18
3. Tell Us More About It (Adjectives) 20
4. How Did You Do That? (Adverbs) 22

C. Mind Quest
1. Roaming Idea Hunt 24
2. Stationary Idea Hunt 26
3. Create A Character 28
4. Create A Place 30

D. Lively Language
1. Simile and the World Similes With You (Comparisons) 32
2. Megawatt Writing 34
3. Understatement 36
4. In Other Words 38

E. Special Features
1. Get a Grip (Titles) 40
2. Opening Hook 42
3. Whose Point of View? 44
4. Let's Talk (Dialogue) 46

F. Even Better: Revision
1. The Minus Sign (Cutting) 48
2. The Plus Sign (Expanding) 50
3. I Can Fix That For You 52
4. Nobody's Perfect 54

Teacher's Guide 56
Problems Chart 82
Strengths Chart 83
Sources of Quotations 84
Meet the Author 86
Permissions Statement 88

How to Use
Igniting Your Writing!

When my husband Dale and I recently moved into the house where I grew up, I found myself surrounded by the familiar books of my childhood. All the Marguerite Henry horse stories, first editions of *Charlotte's Web* and *Stuart Little,* the tan and red "Classics Club" sets which my parents bought month by month, paperback Agatha Christie mysteries, old college literature texts, books of plays, field guides to birds, rocks, trees, and wildflowers—those and hundreds more books overflowed every available shelf. I grew up reading and writing in an atmosphere where words mattered and well-written words were a treasure not to be thrown away.

Igniting Your Writing! came partly from our move into my childhood home and partly from talks with homeschooling parents and teachers in Christian schools. My aims for this writing course are **(1) to encourage young writers; (2) to provide a useful tool for those who teach and encourage young writers.**

What *Igniting Your Writing!* will help you accomplish:

For the hesitant or insecure writer: Many students don't hate writing, but it doesn't come easily or naturally either. *Igniting Your Writing!* gives them competence (they *can* write) and confidence (they *know* they can write). When they have something important to say on paper, they will be able to write it convincingly and well.

For the unwilling writer: These students struggle to put a sentence on paper. We could even call them "non-writers." The lighthearted touch of *Igniting Your Writing!* gently overcomes their resistance. *Start-Up* level of each lesson gives an attainable goal and the reward of a completed result. They did it—and they can do it again!

For the natural writer: These young people are already writing up a storm. Writing is not an assignment they have to finish; it's an inner drive they have to obey. *Igniting Your Writing!* affirms born writers and helps them discipline their natural abilities.

Choose your own level of teacher involvement.
Lesson instructions appear within each lesson. Students can work as independently as you wish. Younger students will sometimes need help with the instructions. You may also choose to be right there with your student at each step of the writing.

The Teacher's Guide beginning on page 56 gives lesson aims, elements to watch for in the student's work, unique features of that lesson, possible pitfalls and solutions, help for evaluating the student's work, and general hints for keeping the young writer writing.

Why aren't the lessons arranged by age or grade?

A student's age or grade often has little relationship to writing ability. Therefore the lessons in *Igniting Your Writing!* are set up not by grade or age but by **writing level**.

Each lesson offers **three options of difficulty:** *Start-Up,* *Intermediate,* **and** *Advanced.* Some 9th graders who have done little writing will need to do *Start-Up* at first. Some 4th graders will be ready for *Intermediate*. A surprisingly wide age range will enjoy *Advanced*. Experiment with different levels for your student. You can even switch back and forth between levels as you work through the book.

Multiple levels mean **more than one student in a family can use** *Igniting Your Writing!* during the same school year. Also **one student can re-use the book** later at a higher level.

And the book stays clean! The student never writes in this book. To help beat the jitters caused by fresh clean paper, **all writing is done on scratch paper.** Scratch paper emphasizes that good writing means rewriting and rewriting again. You can have the student do a final version on good paper if you like.

Flexible schedule.

You may decide to do:
- one lesson per week for most of a school year
- more frequent lessons for a writing unit
- occasional lessons over a longer period of time
- one 4-lesson section, take a break, then another 4-lesson section
- another arrangement which fits your schedule and needs

Lessons in *Igniting Your Writing!* are not sequential. However, the four lessons within each of the six main sections are **closely related and can be used to build on one another.** Section F, "Even Better," makes the most sense if it is done after all or most of the other lessons in the book.

Save all (or as much as you can) of the student's work.
The student will build a very useful idea file, and the final lesson in *Igniting Your Writing!* gives an opportunity to do a major revision of previous work.

A big thank-you to our field testers who gave constructive criticism and helped make *Igniting Your Writing!* a stronger and even more practical teaching tool.

Enjoy *Igniting Your Writing!*

A1
Word Play

Word Trade

This lesson will help you experiment with different word choices.

Todd is a person who doesn't like to write. Yesterday he had this assignment: "Write about what you did last Saturday." He chewed his pencil for a while, then wrote this:

**What I Did Last Saturday
by Todd
I went to the store and got some stuff.**

Well, Todd has made a good *start*. His sentence gets straight to the point. It *answers* several questions: Who? What did he do? Where did he go? It also *raises* questions: Which store? Why that one? What did he get and why? How did he feel about the trip?

Todd thinks he is all done, but when a writer gets words on paper (or on disk), it's only the start. Todd has written a **first draft.** That means it's his first version, his first try. **First drafts are usually not very good, even for the best of writers.** Since it looks like our friend Todd is not going to do a second draft, let alone a third or a fourth, let's continue what he started.

Start-Up:

Take some **unlined** paper which is **already used on one side.** Turn the paper sideways and copy Todd's sentence. Make it fit on one line, but space the words out like this:

    I   went   to   the   store   and   got   some   stuff.

Now play around with the sentence by doing **"word trades."** Here's how: **Cross out "went."** Below it, **write some other possible action words and phrases.** They can be as silly as you like; they just need to be **actions.** For example:

    I ~~went~~ to the store and got some stuff.
       ran
      crawled
   rode my elephant
    pole-vaulted
  walked backwards

Read your new sentences out loud. Now **cross out "got"** and **substitute other action words or phrases.** Examples:

    I ~~went~~ to the store and ~~got~~ some stuff.
                             purchased
                             borrowed
                              grabbed
                             drooled over

Next **cross out "store" and write some *kinds* of stores.** Think of unusual stores as well as the normal types. For example: grocery store, hobby shop, pharmacy, boarded-up store.

Now **cross out "stuff" and write different things you can find at a store.** You may get new ideas for words to put in your other lists. Go ahead and add them too. If you run out of space, get more scratch paper and start the whole thing over!

By now you have what looks like four stacks of words, with Todd's sentence resting on top. What you really have is **a bunch of new sentences which you created.** Read them out loud. You don't have to read straight across; combine the words in different ways.

Congratulations! You kept writing where Todd quit. You also took one boring sentence and turned it into a lot of interesting sentences. (Some of them, the strange ones, may never before have been written by anybody!)

Intermediate:

First do everything under *Start-Up*. Select four of your "word trades" and **write one new sentence** on another piece of scratch paper. If it's funny, that's fine. For example:

> I rode my elephant to the shoe store and grabbed some paper plates.

Add this to the beginning of your sentence: "After _____, . . ."

Add this to the end of your sentence: ". . . . because _____."
(Those are both **dependent clauses.** They cannot stand alone.)

Now **fill in the blank lines.** If your sentence is *too* strange, it may be hard, but try.
Silly answers are easiest, but try to imagine real, *possible* connections.
Write several versions of the sentence.

Take **several more sentences** from your "word trades" list and (again on scratch paper) add "After _____" and "because _____" clauses to them as well.

You have become a storyteller on paper. Each of your new sentences tells a small story, no matter how unusual it is.

Advanced:

Do everything under *Intermediate*. (Yes, first it tells you to do everything under *Start-Up*. It was the only way to fit this lesson on two pages.) Now you have a collection of sentences which begin with "After . . ." and end with "because . . ." Each tells a small one-sentence story.

Choose one of your one-sentence stories and **expand it into a story of several paragraphs.** It will be a challenge if your one-sentence story is rather odd, but keep trying. **Don't let yourself get lazy! Continue to use imaginative and colorful words.** Use lots of scratch paper. Write several versions of the story. If your sentence turns out completely impossible, then choose another and keep going.

A2 Word Play

Sentence Stretch

This lesson will help you smooth out choppy writing by combining short sentences.

When we're in a hurry to write something, we put down as many ideas as possible, as fast as possible. The result is a bunch of short choppy sentences, one idea per sentence. Reading them feels like riding your bike on a railroad or sitting next to a jackhammer—*bam-bam-bam!*

Make life smoother for yourself and for your readers. **Combine a string of short choppy sentences into one or two longer, flowing sentences.**
For example, take these eight short sentences:

> The dog jumped.
> He went into the water.
> There was a big splash.
> The dog swam fast.
> He grabbed the duck.
> He swam back to shore.
> He climbed out of the water.
> He wagged his tail.

We can combine them into one longer sentence like this:

> **New Version #1:** The dog jumped into the water with a big splash and swam fast and grabbed the duck and swam back to shore and climbed out of the water and wagged his tail.

We got rid of the choppiness, but the sentence feels like it's never going to end! Let's try again. We'll combine the eight short sentences into **two sentences:**

> **New Version #2:** The dog jumped into the water with a big splash, swam fast toward the duck, grabbed it and swam back to shore. He climbed out of the water and wagged his tail.

We can also **re-arrange the ideas** as we make two new sentences:

> **New Version #3:** There was a big splash as the dog jumped into the water and swam fast toward the duck. He grabbed it and swam back to shore, climbed out and wagged his tail.

Start-Up:

Now you try! Read these seven short choppy sentences:

> She threw the egg.
> She threw it really hard.
> The egg was raw.
> It hit my forehead.
> It went SPLAT!
> I thought she was my friend.
> I found out I was wrong.

On scratch paper, make those seven short sentences into one or two longer sentences. (No fair just putting commas in place of the periods!) You don't have to write a whole new story, but do include all the facts from the short sentences. Re-arrange some ideas if you want. For example, you can write "she threw the *raw* egg."

Read your writing out loud. Does your version **feel and sound better and smoother** than our seven short sentences? If you don't think so, **write another version (a second draft).** Writers usually write a *lot* of versions (drafts) before they get the one they want!

Intermediate:

Read everything under *Start-Up*. Take the seven sentences about the egg and **rewrite them as one or two longer sentences.** Come up with **at least three new versions.**

Read your new versions out loud to test their smoothness. Which version do you think is best? Circle it, then **write a short explanation of why you think it's the best.**

Advanced:

Read everything under *Start-Up*. **Make up** between six and nine short choppy sentences of your own. **Combine** them into one or two longer, more flowing sentences. Come up with **five new versions.** One version must include a **question.** Read them aloud to test their flow.

Make notes about *why* you think your newer versions feel more satisfying both to write and to read. **Choose** your best version. Now **rewrite it** to try to make it feel even more satisfying.

A3 Word Play

Sentence Shrink

This lesson will help you shorten sentences which are too long.

Some writers are afraid to end a sentence. They don't know where to stop, so they add words and more words and hope the problem goes away. If you did Lesson A2 "Sentence Stretch," you read a sentence which goes on so long, you wish you'd brought a sandwich:

"The dog jumped into the water with a big splash and swam fast and grabbed the duck and swam back to shore and climbed out of the water and wagged his tail."

Here's an even longer sentence:

You may not believe this, but yesterday a space ship swooped down over my back yard and hovered for a while before it landed and a door opened, a ladder popped out and a Martian with six arms and two heads stood at the doorway, and was I ever scared, and when it saw me it pulled the ladder up and went back inside and took off and by the way, have you looked out your window?

We say a sentence like that one *rambles*. It's a *rambling sentence*. A rambling sentence goes on and on and on. Rambling sentences can be fun, but too many of them strain your reader's brain. Just as an endless road exhausts a traveler, rambling sentences exhaust your reader.

A rambling sentence is not the same as a run-on sentence. A run-on sentence is an incorrect sentence; it's several sentences stuck together with commas between them or with no punctuation at all between them. Our rambling space ship sentence is correct, but it is not very good writing. *You* are going to fix that!

Start-Up:

On scratch paper, take our rambling sentence about the space ship and **turn it into at least four shorter sentences.** Try to include *all* the facts *and* the question at the end.

Intermediate:

On scratch paper, add some facts to our rambling sentence about the space ship and rewrite the sentence so it is *even longer* (if you can stand it). Now take your new super-rambling sentence and **rewrite it as at least four shorter sentences.** You can decide whether to include the question at the end.

Advanced:

Not every long sentence is a rambling sentence. Some sentences need to be long. A good writer knows *why* a sentence requires a certain overgrown length. **A sentence can be fairly lengthy, as long as it keeps its focus.**

Here is an example of a good long sentence from *The Code of the Woosters* by P. G. Wodehouse. The narrator Bertie Wooster explains his reaction to the sight of his friend Gussie Fink-Nottle crawling out from under a bed:

> Owing to the fact that the shock had caused my tongue to get tangled up with my tonsils, inducing an unpleasant choking sensation, I found myself momentarily incapable of speech.

That sentence is long, but it does not ramble. The author knows where he is going and has a definite purpose. The sentence is exactly as long as it needs to be. Sure, Bertie could have said, "I was so shocked, I couldn't talk for a minute." However, that isn't how Bertie Wooster says things. The sentence is consistent with the narrator's style.

You don't need to shrink a sentence like that one. You should shrink a sentence which rambles on and on for no discernible purpose.

On scratch paper, **write five sentences which are long but do not ramble.** Hint: decide on your purpose for a long sentence **before** you start to write.

A4 Word Play

Flip It! (Word Order)

This lesson will help you make different parts of a sentence important by changing the word order.

Suppose you write a perfectly good sentence. It's correct. It makes sense. Still it doesn't *feel* right to you. Your #1 idea does not come out as #1; it gets lost. How can you fix it?

One way to make an idea important is to put it at the end of your sentence. Example:

>A herd of buffalo ran down the hill straight toward me.

The emphasis is on "straight toward me." It grabs the reader's attention. Unless you own a herd of pet buffalo and have just called them for dinner, you're in a dangerous situation!

Suppose we flip the sentence around and put the buffalo at the end:

>Down the hill straight toward me ran a herd of buffalo.

Now the buffalo are the stars of the sentence. At the beginning, the reader knows only that something ran down the hill toward the writer. It could be children, mice, sheep, even a road. At the end, the reader discovers it's a herd of buffalo. The mood of the sentence takes a jolt from casual to alarming.

Suppose we flip the sentence around a different way:

>Straight toward me a herd of buffalo ran down the hill.

That sentence does not feel as strong as the other two versions. "Down the hill" is now most important, but a hill does not have the emotional punch of "a herd of buffalo" or "straight toward me." **However, the writer may have a good reason to emphasize the hill.** Maybe this is the first line of a story called "The Hill" about events which happened on this particular hill.

Next, let's take a quote:

>"I have no idea what she meant by that remark."

"That remark" (whatever it was) is the important feature of the sentence. In your head you can even hear the speaker stress *"that remark."* Let's flip the quote around:

>"What she meant by that remark, I have no idea."

This time the emphasis is on **the speaker's ignorance.** The speaker does not know (and probably does not care) what was meant by "that remark."

When you change the word order of a sentence, you may have to change the form of a word to keep it correct. Take this sentence:

> Good days and bad days come to everybody's life.

You can change the emphasis to "good days and bad days" this way:

> To everybody's life come good days and bad days.

But suppose you want to emphasize "everybody." You need to change "everybody's life" to "the life of everybody:"

> Good days and bad days come to the life of everybody.

Start-Up:

Look through some of your favorite books. Pick out at least three sentences and write each on a separate piece of scratch paper. **See how many ways you can flip each sentence around to change what is most important in the sentence.** Sometimes your new sentence may feel clumsy. It's OK to cross it out and try again. You're learning to tell your not-so-good writing from your good writing.

Intermediate:

On scratch paper, write an original sentence. (Note the emphasis is on "original sentence." If we had said "Write an original sentence on scratch paper" . . . but you know that already.) Now **flip the words around to emphasize a different part of your sentence. Write at least four new versions.**

Advanced:

Flipping the word order of sentences is like turning somersaults. A few are OK; too many make you dizzy. A reader is confused by page after page of sentences with flip-flopped word order.

Here's a paragraph written in unusual word order. Read through it carefully and decide what ideas you would like to emphasize. Work out which sentences to flip around and which to leave as they are. **Write out a new, revised paragraph on scratch paper.** If you aren't happy with it, rewrite it a couple of times until you are satisfied with the emphasis of each sentence.

> Between the islands of St. Thomas and St. John, overboard the pirates threw me. Above my head the cold salt water closed. Up I came coughing and gagging. Left, right, and behind me frantically I looked for help. Forward at last I turned my desperate gaze. Almost could I not believe that through the air flew a long jagged board. With a cold splash which slapped my face a yard from me it struck the water. Frantically I flailed my arms and kicked until the rough wood was clutched by my stiff fingers. To the faces of the pirates went my gaze upward. Not quite as cruel as the others was one face. That face would I forget never.

B1 Parts of Speech

Action! (Verbs)

This lesson will help you choose strong verbs so the action of your writing comes alive for the reader.

Verbs seem easy. Any writer can come up with a verb. However, a thoughtful writer crosses out a lot of verbs before the right one comes along—and often the writer feels there's still a better verb, a perfect verb, out there somewhere.

A good verb helps your reader see and feel the action.

It's easy to write **"She walked home."** But how many ways are there to walk? "She walked home" does not give your reader a clear look at *how* she walked home. Watch what happens when you use a different verb: **She strolled, stumbled, staggered, wandered, rushed, hiked, marched, strutted.** Each of those verbs shows a different way to walk. Each verb plants a different picture and a different feeling in the reader's mind.

In his book *Travels with Charley,* John Steinbeck writes of his trip across the U.S. in a truck named Rocinante. His dog Charley came along. In the Badlands of South Dakota, they meet a rough-looking hunter. Steinbeck writes:

> I pulled up to speak to him, saw his eyes wash over Rocinante, sweep up the details, and then retire into their sockets.

A weaker writer would have had the hunter's eyes "look over Rocinante, notice the details, and then go back into their sockets." With the verbs **wash over, sweep up** and **retire,** Steinbeck shows us the hunter's scorn for him and his truck—and probably for his dog too.

To choose a strong verb, you need to see and feel the action yourself (at least in your mind).

In my *Jackpine Point Adventure* #1, *The Re-Appearing Statue,* I needed some good verbs for a complex chain of events. Here's the set-up: The five friends hold a meeting in the attic of Dillon's home. The floor of the attic has three trap doors with ladders down into three different rooms. David Malloy, holding a Little League trophy behind his back, backs up and falls through one of the holes. Here's the final sentence from the book:

> One foot went down into space, the other foot followed, one hand grabbed for the edge of the hole, the other hand still clutched the trophy, and I dangled from one elbow which was hooked onto the attic floor while my feet fumbled for the ladder.

My first ten or eleven tries at that sentence were a mess. I did not understand exactly what happens when you step backward through a trap door with one hand full, and I didn't want to try it personally. With my husband's help, I acted it out (minus a real hole in the floor) until I got the right actions in the right order.

Start-Up:

The following sentences have weak verbs in *italics*. On scratch paper, **rewrite each sentence using a stronger verb.** Try several verbs until you find one that does the job well. **Act out** the sentences if it helps you. (Yes, you can act like a hurricane as long as you don't break anything.) You may need to add other words to a verb to complete your idea. For example, for sentence #2, instead of "touched" you could write "slammed into."

1. Peter "Lightpaw" Peterson, master spy, *walked* toward enemy headquarters.
2. The hurricane *touched* the fishing boats.
3. My rescuers *threw* me a life preserver, and I *caught* it.
4. When my name was *spoken* for the top award, I *went* to the platform.
5. After a week in the desert, I *drank* a lot of water at an oasis.

Intermediate:

Each of the following sentences desperately needs a few good verbs. **Rewrite each sentence on scratch paper, using the best verbs you can find.** When you have filled in verbs for each sentence, go back and try to find **even better verbs** for the blanks.

1. As the heavy rain began, I _____ into my tent and _____ there through the long cold night.

2. I called the police and _____ them to _____ immediately because a strange person was _____ around my house.

3. When the singer _____ the high note, I _____ my ears because I didn't want my eardrums to _____.

4. We _____ through the old trunk until we _____ the letters, _____ them out and _____them so we could _____ our ancestor's Civil War record.

5. I _____ through my schoolwork so I could _____ out into the warm sunshine and _____the rest of the day.

Advanced:

Here is an excerpt from my *Jackpine Point Adventure #3, Something's Fishy*. Verbs are in *italics*. The narrator, David Malloy, is about to go on a canoe trip. David's mood is generally optimistic. **Rewrite the excerpt** by substituting verbs which **change the narrator's mood to fear and dread of the trip.** You may want to keep some verbs as they are. You can change other details to increase the sense of apprehension; for example, you might want to alter those calm blue waters and light green trees.

> We *tumbled* out of the cars to *stand* on a paved parking lot where a boat ramp *sloped* down to calm blue waters *ringed* by spruce and pine and aspen trees, which *were wearing* their early light spring green. The lake *looked* small, but the adults *said* we *were* only *seeing* one end of it. It was supposed to *lengthen* to the right around a bend in the shore. We *would paddle* that way to our first campsite at the far end of this lake. The days *are getting* long up here this time of year so we *would have* plenty of daylight *to make* it.

17

B2
Parts of Speech

What *Is* This? (Nouns)

This lesson will help you choose clear, definite nouns.

"A noun is a person, place, or thing." I learned that definition long ago. Of course a *noun* is not a person, place, or thing. A noun is only a *word* for a person, place, or thing. While you know which person, place, or thing you mean, your reader does not necessarily know.

Suppose I write you a letter which says, "I took my cat to the pet show." You read the noun "cat" and picture a cute little orange-and-white kitten. Then a photo of me and my cat falls out of the envelope. My cat is a huge Persian with long silky white hair and a bored expression. **My noun "cat" did not tell you enough.** (At least it was a better noun than "animal," which would have told you even less.)

The great little book about writing, Strunk and White's *The Elements of Style,* says that the best way to grab and hold your reader's attention is to be "specific, definite, and concrete." In other words, say what you mean as exactly as possible. **The right noun** helps you do that.

Start-Up:

Take a look at the following lists. The list on the left has very general nouns. Each noun could mean a lot of different things. The nouns in the middle list narrow down the meaning somewhat. **Copy these lists onto scratch paper. Complete the right-hand list with nouns which are even more exact.** The first three examples will get you started.

driver	NASCAR driver	Dale Earnhardt
reptile	snake	python
competition	athletics	Olympics
weather	storm	
tree	evergreen	
food	dessert	
clothing	footwear	
relative	grandparent	
machine	computer	

Intermediate:

Here is a fuller quote from *The Elements of Style:* "Prefer the specific to the general, the definite to the vague, the concrete to the abstract."

Suppose you write "They turned onto the highway." You realize that the noun *highway* is too general, vague, and abstract. It could mean anything from a jammed interstate to a lonely country road. You revise the sentence to "They turned onto the *interstate*" because *interstate* is more **specific, definite, and concrete.** Your reader will see *interstate* and think of multiple lanes of heavy high-speed traffic. If your characters are driving from Minneapolis to Duluth, you could even write "They turned onto *Interstate 35-W.*"

Use the rule of "specific, definite, and concrete" with common sense. **Sometimes a general noun is your best choice.** It makes sense to write "When I was a kid I was hit by a car." The *kind* of car does not matter; what matters is that you were hit. If you write, "When I was a kid I was hit by a red Ford Windstar minivan," the reader expects the red Ford Windstar minivan to be important to the rest of the story. If it is, fine. If it isn't, why pin it down?

For most of the nouns in the following paragraph, we provide three choices, from general to more specific to quite specific. A few modifiers have been added to keep the grammar correct. **Write out the paragraph on scratch paper, choosing your nouns as you go. Read through your new paragraph and make any changes which feel right.** Make notes about *why* you chose each of your nouns.

When I woke up on (that day / Saturday / Saturday, November 13), I had no idea of the (event / problem / danger) which waited for me. I pulled on (pants / jeans / work jeans) and my souvenir (top / shirt / Florida t-shirt) and ran downstairs to eat my usual (breakfast / cereal / Wheaties). My mouth was full when I heard a (sound / knocking / banging) on the door. I swallowed the rest of my (food / breakfast / cereal) and hurried to open the door. There stood (a person / a friend / Maggie). "When did you get back?" she demanded. " (The other day / Thursday / Thursday, November 11th)," I said with (emotion / worry / dread). Not only had I neglected to call her when I got back; I had forgotten to send her a (communication / message / postcard) while I was on my trip. I was now under Maggie's sentence of (disapproval / rejection / condemnation) and I would stay there for the next (period of time / several days / week).

Advanced:

In *The Elements of Style,* Strunk and White advise the writer to "prefer the specific to the general, the definite to the vague, the concrete to the abstract." When you write about an unusual or technical subject, you will be tempted to use nouns which are so specific, definite, and concrete that **your reader has no idea what you mean.** Still, **a technical noun is sometimes the right noun for the job,** even if the reader does not know its precise definition.

Read this passage from *The Open Boat Across the Pacific* by Webb Chiles:

Chidiock's jib sheet was still tied to the tiller, but she could not steer herself without yawing madly, and I was controlling the helm. I wanted to reduce sail but did not dare leave the tiller. A great shrieking gust made the decision for me by laying us over until the starboard gunwale was beneath the water. I leaped for the main halyard and gratefully watched the gaff slide down. Securing the mainsail, I let *Chidiock* rest under backed jib and mizzen.

Unless you're a sailor, you probably don't have enough fingers to count all the nouns in that passage which you don't understand (plus some verbs and adjectives). But **you still get the picture:** a sailboat is in trouble and the sailor has to take quick action!

Pick a subject with which you are familiar, but which requires **nouns which the uninitiated would not understand. Write a paragraph similar to the sailing excerpt.** Use your special terms in a way which communicates your meaning, even if the reader does not own a technical dictionary of the subject.

Tell Us More About It (Adjectives)

B3 Parts of Speech

This lesson will help you use adjectives to sharpen the meanings of your nouns.

An adjective modifies a noun. **It narrows down a noun which is too general**—that is, a noun which is too wide-reaching with too many possible meanings. For example, suppose I write:

In the middle of our woods stands a tree.

My noun "tree" is **too general.** It could mean any tree in the middle part of our woods. Of course I don't mean just any tree; I mean a *certain* tree. So I **narrow it down:**

In the middle of our woods stands a sycamore.

"Sycamore" is a very **specific** (narrow) noun. It's fine—*if* the reader knows what a sycamore is. Suppose the reader doesn't know, or suppose I am not sure if the reader knows. I can describe the tree in more detail:

In the middle of our woods stands a tree with bark and leaves.

That doesn't help much. The nouns *bark* and *leaves* are almost as general as the noun *tree*. I need to find a **middle ground** between **nouns which are too general** and **nouns which are too specific.** So I add **adjectives (they're in *italics*):**

In the middle of our woods stands a *giant* tree with *smooth creamy* bark and *huge five-pointed* leaves.

I could say a lot more about that tree, but my adjectives communicate at least some idea of what a sycamore is. If I decide the reader needs to learn the word "sycamore," I can write the sentence this way:

In the middle of our woods stands a sycamore, a giant tree with smooth creamy bark and huge five-pointed leaves.

If your noun isn't doing the job for you, try adding an adjective. However, don't drag in piles of adjectives to prop up a weak noun. Often what you need is not a string of adjectives but a more specific noun. (See Lesson B2 on Nouns.) **Adjectives will strengthen your writing when you know clearly why you choose and use each one.**

In the Sherlock Holmes stories, Arthur Conan Doyle chose strong adjectives to describe his settings and characters. In this excerpt from *The Adventure of the Speckled Band,* a woman comes to ask the great detective for help. She is dressed in black, with a heavy veil over her face. *Adjectives* are in *italics:*

20

> She raised her veil as she spoke, and we could see that she was indeed in a *pitiable* state of agitation, her face all *drawn* and *grey,* with *restless, frightened* eyes, like those of some *hunted* animal. Her features and figure were those of a woman of thirty, but her hair was shot with *premature* grey, and her expression was *weary* and *haggard.* Sherlock Holmes ran her over with one of his *quick, all-comprehensive* glances.

Even if some of those adjectives sent you to the dictionary (good!) you get a vivid picture of Sherlock Holmes' visitor.

Start-Up:

Imagine a stranger who comes to visit you, as the veiled woman came to visit Sherlock Holmes. **Write a description of the imaginary person, but** *don't use any adjectives.* We use adjectives so naturally when we talk or write that you'll find it hard to write without them! Then **rewrite the description with adjectives added.** Make the adjectives as descriptive as possible.

Intermediate:

Adjectives can be powerful mood-setters. Read this excerpt from *A Separate Peace* by John Knowles. The teenage narrator Gene lives at Devon, a New England boarding school, at the beginning of World War II. His best friend Phineas has been injured in a fall from a tree. Gene is tortured with guilt because he deliberately bounced the branch which made Phineas fall. He does not know if Phineas knows. To escape his problem, Gene considers enlisting in the Army:

> It was a night made for hard thoughts. Sharp stars pierced singly through the blackness, not sweeps of them or clusters or Milky Ways as there might have been in the South, but single, chilled points of light, as unromantic as knife blades. Devon, muffled under the gentle occupation of the snow, was dominated by them; the cold Yankee stars ruled this night. They did not invoke in me thoughts of God, or sailing before the mast, or some great love as crowded night skies at home had done; I thought instead, in the light of those cold points, of the decision facing me.

On scratch paper **write all the adjectives you find in the excerpt** (except *a, the, this* or *those*). Describe the **mood** of the excerpt. Make notes about how the author uses adjectives to establish the mood. **Rewrite the paragraph with different adjectives** to establish a sense of **warmth and optimism** in Gene. (You do not have to change every adjective.)

Advanced:

Study the excerpt from *A Separate Peace* under *Intermediate*. **List the adjectives** in the excerpt (except *a, the, this* or *those*). **Make notes** about how the adjectives help establish a particular mood.

Write an original paragraph using adjectives to set a mood similar to the mood of the excerpt from *A Separate Peace*. Consider how different adjectives would alter the emotional feel of your paragraph. **Rewrite your paragraph to change the adjectives and set a different mood** which you choose. (You do not have to change every adjective.)

B4 Parts of Speech

How Did You Do That? (Adverbs)

This lesson will help you use adverbs wisely and not too much.

Our community theatre group was practicing a play. A new actor had joined the cast. He did fine until the middle of one scene, when he waved his arms and shouted, "I have ABSOLUTELY, POSITIVELY, COMPLETELY, TOTALLY, no idea what is going on!"

The actor could have said, "I have no idea what is going on." He got his message across with much more power because he used **adverbs: "absolutely, positively, completely, totally.**"

An adverb usually modifies a verb. It answers certain questions which a verb leaves unanswered: "How?" "When?" "Where?" "How much?"
An adverb can also modify an adjective or another adverb. It answers the questions "How?" "How much?" "To what extent?"

In these examples, **adverbs are in *italics*. The words they modify are <u>underlined</u>.**

Jesus *often* <u>went</u> *somewhere* <u>to pray</u> *alone*.
    The adverbs *often* and *somewhere* modify the verb <u>went</u>.
        Often answers the question "When?"
        Somewhere answers the question "Where?"
    The adverb *alone* modifies the verb <u>to pray</u>.
        Alone answers the question "How?"

Take one pill *before* every meal.
    The adverb *before* modifies the adjective <u>every</u>.
        Before answers the question "When?"

I <u>enjoy</u> cooking spaghetti *very much*, but I <u>like</u> eating it *even more*.
    The adverb *very* modifies the adverb *much*, which modifies the verb <u>enjoy</u>.
    The adverb *even* modifies the adverb *more*, which modifies the verb <u>like</u>.
    Very, much, even, and *more* all answer the question "To what extent?"

It's easy to make an adverb: take an adjective and add -*ly*. *Quick* becomes *quickly*, *careful* becomes *carefully*, *amazing* becomes *amazingly*, *simple* becomes *simply*, *happy* becomes *happily*. (As you can see, sometimes the spelling changes.)

Not every adverb ends in -*ly*. *Seldom, never, always, again, not, never, while,* and *once* are common adverbs.

Not every word which ends in -*ly* is an adverb. *Silly, butterfly, family,* and *Emily* are not adverbs! If you can chop off the -*ly* and have an adjective left, you have an adverb.

22

Start-Up:

In the following sentences, think of **an adverb for each blank.** Don't settle for the first one which comes to you. Try to find some more unusual possibilities. **On scratch paper, write each sentence with adverbs filled in:**

1. I picked up my half-written story _____ and read it over _____ before I stuffed it _____ into a drawer.

2. "I can _____ beat you at tennis!" he said _____ as he _____ tossed his racket into the air.

3. When I _____ put on my costume and found that it fit me _____, I thought of how _____ I had agreed to be in this play.

Intermediate:

Read the following excerpt from *The Northern Lights: Lighthouses of the Upper Great Lakes.* **Find the adverbs** and write them on scratch paper. Next to each adverb, **write the word which it modifies.** Note whether the modified word is a **verb, adjective, or other adverb.**

On December 5, 1906, the Canadian passenger ship *Monarch* was driven aground off Isle Royale by a violent snowstorm. The forty-one people aboard managed to get ashore, but had no food or shelter and suffered badly. They were able to start a fire and luckily, on their third day marooned on the island, a bag of flour washed ashore and they made some bread. . . . Dozens and dozens of less dramatic rescues were common, but rarely received much attention. . . . A lightkeeper or a member of his family rescued someone on the Great Lakes nearly every year and they saved thousands of lives simply keeping their lights and fog signals in service.

Advanced:

Because it's so easy to make adverbs, lazy writers overuse them. In Lesson B3 on adjectives, we advise writers not to use adjectives to prop up a weak noun. The same goes for adverbs. Don't use adverbs to prop up a weak verb, adjective, or other weak adverb. It's better to substitute a different, more definite word.

Read this annoying adverb-heavy paragraph. Each italicized phrase is an adverb plus the word it modifies. **Rewrite the paragraph to replace each phrase with one definite and vivid word.**

Curlyhorn, *very powerful* and *really tough* general of the beetle army, *proceeded sneakily* along the *extremely dirty* sidewalk of Main Street. A squad of beetle soldiers *marched behind* him. Night *had passed quickly,* and dawn was *speedily coming.* Taxicabs *honked loudly* as they *drove noisily* past. Their exhaust made the beetles *breathe chokingly.* Curlyhorn *stopped suddenly.* His feelers *moved unevenly* through the air. He *said loudly,* "Who *foolishly tries* to challenge the Great Army of the Beetles?" Ahead a lone bug *crawled painfully* toward them. A beetle soldier *exclaimed surprisedly,* "General, it's our *truly brave* scout Hardback! He's been *badly harmed!*" Hardback *came haltingly* to General Curlyhorn, saluted with one *grievously damaged* leg, and *fell heavily.*

C1 Mind Quest

Roaming Idea Hunt

This lesson will help you find and capture new writing ideas.

"I want to write, but I don't know what to write *about*."
The young person who said that was ready and willing to write. She only needed ideas. Even one idea would have given her a place to start.

That young writer actually had tons of ideas available. She worked at a summer camp on a small lake. Every week one army of kids left and a new mob arrived. The camp had been on that beautiful wooded lakeshore for 75 years. Surrounded by people, history, and nature, she still could not find anything to write about!

It reminds me of an old recipe for tiger stew. The recipe begins: **"First, catch a tiger."** The young writer at camp wanted to make tiger stew, but she needed to go out and catch a tiger. **Ideas were all around her; she only needed to capture one idea and hold it down long enough to write about it.**

How does a writer capture ideas?
If you want to catch a tiger, you have to go to its natural habitat. What is the natural habitat of ideas? Writers are lucky. **Ideas are everywhere!** Once you start to see them, you'll no longer ask, "How do I get ideas?" You'll ask, "What do I do with all these ideas I've caught?" You won't even have to hunt for them. They'll jump out of the brush and pounce on you!

Start-Up:

Grab paper and pencil. They're your best equipment for an idea hunt. A notebook or legal pad is good because it gives you a firm surface on which to write.

With your parent/teacher, set yourself a **time limit**.
With your paper and pencil, roam around indoors or outdoors, look everywhere and **write down anything and everything you notice in some special or unusual way**—anything that grabs your attention. Don't try to write a whole story. Just jot down words and phrases.

Much of what you write down will come from **outside you**, as you observe with your five senses: seeing, hearing, touching, smelling and tasting. (Don't taste anything unless you know it's safe!) What grabs your attention? What makes you turn around for a second look or listen or sniff? What makes you lean closer to overhear?

When time is up, come back to your starting point and **read over your notes. Circle** ones you especially like. **Draw an arrow** to one in particular which you think *could* be made into a good paragraph or even a story.

Save all your notes, because you may use them later—even years from now!*

Intermediate:

Do everything under *Start-Up,* with this addition: Some of what you write down will come from **inside you**, from your memories. Maybe something you see reminds you of something that happened, pleasant or unpleasant. Ask yourself: What keeps stirring me? Who or what am I reminded of continually or often? What nags my mind?

When you reach the end of your time limit, come back to your starting point and read everything over. **Choose one idea and expand it into a paragraph.** Read through your paragraph and **rewrite it to improve it.**

Save all your notes!

Advanced:

Do everything under *Start-Up* **and** *Intermediate.*

Now try to tie several of your notes together into a story or article of at least four paragraphs. Don't force yourself to use every idea; you probably can't. Think of the ideas you gathered during your Idea Hunt as a treasure chest of possibilities. Pull out and use what you can now. Save the rest for another time.

* Ideas "keep" better and longer than any food will ever keep in your freezer! A good idea is practically timeless. I have pulled ideas out of a file and used them YEARS after I stored them away—not because I was desperate, but because the idea suddenly fit.

For example, the title of Lesson D1 in this book is "Simile and the World Similes With You." Originally that was a line from a play which I wrote *14 years* before I wrote this curriculum. I always liked the line, and it was time to use it again.

C2
Mind Quest

Stationary Idea Hunt

This lesson will help you notice ideas which are right in front of you.

Bird hunters hunt in different ways, depending on what kind of birds they are after. Grouse hunters stalk slowly through the woods and the fields. Duck hunters sit in one spot and wait for their prey to fly by.

Wouldn't you expect duck hunters to get bored? They sit there in a boat or in a duck blind (a camouflaged shelter) and wait . . . and wait . . . and wait. They look like they're doing nothing. In fact they stay very busy. **They watch. They listen. They pay attention.**

We writers sometimes feel like we're sitting in a duck blind. Life goes along. Nothing much happens. We can't find many good ideas to write about. But ideas *will* land right in front of us, if we are patient and **watch, listen and pay attention!**

If you did Lesson C1 "Roaming Idea Hunt," you went out and stalked ideas the way a grouse hunter stalks grouse. In this lesson you will **hunt for ideas duck-hunter style.**

Start-Up:

Choose a place to sit. Think of it as your "idea blind" (like a duck blind). It can be indoors or outdoors, quiet or noisy. There are only 3 rules about this place:

1. It should not be totally silent.
2. It should be away from the sound of TV, radio, tapes etc.
3. It should not be where you can see or smell food.

Get paper and pencil. If you are not going to sit at a table, use a notebook or legal pad to give you a firm surface on which to write.

With your parent/teacher, **set a time limit for yourself.** We suggest less than 5 minutes. You can set a timer, but if you hear it ticking away, it may distract you too much.

As you sit there in your chosen spot, look around. Close your eyes for part of the time and **listen**. What do you notice? What happens? What are you reminded of? What sounds grab your attention? How do you feel? Is it cold? Hot? Breathe deeply—any unusual scents? **Write down anything and everything which catches your attention.**

On the next page are some examples of "ducks" which may fly by (the kind of notes you might make):

- Light patch moves on floor as wind blows trees outside window
- Refrigerator sounds like old car — reminds me of story I read
- Somebody's whining, complaining
- Lots of different shades of red in this room — how many?
- I can feel each toe pressing against inside of my shoe

Now move to a different spot and do your Idea Hunt again. Your time limit can be shorter, longer, or the same.

Now do the Idea Hunt once more . . . but go back to your first spot. Your eyes and ears will pick up things you missed in that spot the first time.

That's it! Save your "ducks" (your notes). You will likely use them as writing ideas later.

Intermediate:

Do everything under *Start-Up,* except allow yourself at least 10 minutes for each hunt. (Longer is fine.) **For your third hunt,** *don't* **go back to your first spot;** *stay* **in your second spot.**

After each hunt, when your time is up, make these additional notes:

What **ordinary** things came alive to you in some new way?
What happened that was **unexpected?**

Save all your notes!

Advanced:

Do everything under *Intermediate.*

Choose one of your ideas (or several which you can tie together) and expand your idea(s) into a **story or article of at least four paragraphs.** As with the Roaming Idea Hunt (Lesson C1), don't expect to use every idea you gathered. You probably can't. Pull out and use the ideas which fit right now, and save the rest for another time.

Create A Character

C3 Mind Quest

This lesson will help you create characters your reader cares about.

Think of a boring story you have read or a boring movie or TV show you have seen. Why was it boring?

A story can have action, beautiful descriptions and a worthwhile message—yet it still bores you. You don't care about what happens next.

What drives a story forward and pulls the reader along? It isn't so much the "what" or the "when" or even the "why" of the story. It's the **"who." When the reader cares about a story's characters, the reader cares what happens next.**

    If you want to write an interesting story, create (or find) interesting characters.

Where do writers get their characters? A strong character often comes from someone the writer knows. A writer may mix several people together to create one character. The writer's own personality sometimes goes into a character (though the writer may not admit it). And of course a character can be a real person. No matter whether real or imagined . . .

    A character must be able to make decisions.
    That is, **a character must be able to choose what to do next.** Here's why:

A character in a story always wants something. It can be a material thing like land or money. It can be a better relationship: family, romantic, friendship, or with God. It can be an inner feeling like happiness, pride, or revenge. The story unfolds as the character goes after the goal.

Along the way, **the character meets obstacles**. An obstacle is a problem or a roadblock which threatens to keep him from his goal. Anything can come up as an obstacle:

- another character in the story
- a circumstance such as accident or illness
- nature (such as storm, wilderness, flood, desert)
- the character's own weakness or fear

The obstacle makes the character struggle on the inside and maybe on the outside. When the obstacle comes up, the character **must decide what to do next.** That decision pushes the story's action in a slightly different direction—while the character still aims for the final goal. **That's why your character must be able to make decisions. Take away the power of choice from your character, and your story falls flat.**

Characters are the "people" in your story, but they **do not have to be human beings.** A character can be an animal, an alien from another planet, or a fantasy creature. Even a tree or a rock can be a character, but not if it just sits there being a tree or a rock. The writer must give it a personality so it can think, feel, and—most important—**make decisions.**

During the story, a character **changes** in some way: grows better or worse, more hopeful or less hopeful, more trusting or more suspicious . . . the possibilities go on and on. By the end of the story, the character has either reached the goal or has not. Maybe he gets what he wants but decides it isn't what he wants after all!

Start-Up:

Begin to make up a character. You don't need to have a story in mind; just begin to invent a character. Try to understand this person you have created as well as possible. On scratch paper, **answer these questions** to help you get started:

> How would you describe this character's looks? (male or female, age, face, size)
> What is the character's name? If it's a nickname, how did the character get it?
> What are the character's strengths? weaknesses?
> What does this character want? (short-term and long-term)
> How does this character wish he or she were different?
> Would you know this character if you met him or her on the street?

Experiment with different answers to the questions. **Keep your notes** so you can keep developing this character. A story does not have to mention all the facts you know about your character, but *you* need to know them. **If you don't know your character person well, you might have him or her suddenly do something "out of character"—something which that person would never do. Your readers will stop believing you.**

Intermediate:

Do the *Start-Up* activity with these additional questions about your character:

> How would you describe the character's outlook on life?
> What is the character's background (past)?
> What does the character hope for the future?
> What is important to this character? What doesn't matter?

Advanced:

Do *Intermediate*. Now **begin to develop a story** about the character you have invented. Plant some **obstacles** in your character's way. **What does your character decide to do** about those obstacles? The character's decisions will begin to give you a story.
Keep your notes so you can continue to work on the possibilities of a story or stories based on this character.

C4 Mind Quest

Create A Place

This lesson will help you invent fascinating settings for stories.

We writers are lucky. We can live *anywhere*, at least in our minds.

Do you want to live in a castle? in a cabin in the woods? in a hut on a beach? in a treehouse? on another planet? How about at the bottom of the ocean? Or just in another state?

The place where a story or an article happens is called its **setting.** Some settings are real, some are imaginary, and many are a combination of the two.

Start-Up:

Imagine what your life would be like if you lived in one of these places:

- a tree house
- a cave
- a mansion
- a beach house
- a sphere at the bottom of the ocean
- a cabin with no electricity or running water
- a caretaker's house in an amusement park
- an abandoned building

Choose one of those settings and write a **careful and complete description** of your home. (It may help if you draw pictures of your home first. The pictures don't have to be great art. They're only to help you see the place in your mind.) Explain your daily routine in this place. Mention any special problems and any special advantages which come with living there.

Intermediate:

Choose a place you know well. It can be anywhere: your room, your yard, the place you do your schoolwork, a friend's front porch, your favorite aisle in the grocery store, a place your family visits often, or anywhere else. It could even be a place with unpleasant associations, such as a hospital room where you spent too much time.

Imagine you have a pen pal in a very different part of the world. **Write a letter** to your pen pal describing your chosen place. You may need to explain certain terms or the use of certain objects. (For purposes of this exercise, assume that your pen pal knows English well.)

If you normally keep in touch with faraway friends by e-mail, you can write your letter as an e-mail, then print it out.

Advanced:

Do the *Intermediate* activity. Then imagine that your pen pal receives your letter and writes you a letter in return, describing a familiar setting in his or her own world. **Write that letter to yourself from your pen pal, with this condition: your pen pal lives in an entirely fictional place which you must invent.** Make notes on the characteristics of this place: climate, land formations, style of homes, population density, how modern or undeveloped it is, values which the people hold, type of government, medium of exchange (money, trade etc.), typical foods, typical dress, and any other features which are important.

In your letter "from" your pen pal, you will probably not mention all those details. You should still get a handle on them, so you have a clear picture in your own mind of the place you invent. Maybe you'll want to take a vacation there!

D1
Lively Language

Simile and the World Similes With You (Comparisons)

This lesson will help you write colorful comparisons.

How often do you hear the word "like"? Probably too often. Some people use "like" as another way of saying "uh" or "um." ("Like, I heard what she said and like, how could she say that, because, like, we were like best friends.")

If we don't mistreat it, *like* is a useful and even powerful word.

When you say something is **like** something else, you make a **simile** (SIM-ih-lee). A **simile** says **something is *similar to* something else.** Even if you didn't KNOW the word "simile," you already USE similes all the time. Do these sound familiar?

"Slow down! When you run down those steps, it feels **like an earthquake**."
"Talking to her is **like talking to a brick wall**."

A simile does not have to include the word "like," so long as it has the *idea* of likeness. "You're **as good as gold**" and "I feel **as a big as a house**" are similes.

Any writer can think of a tired-out, overused simile. A thoughtful writer comes up with original similes which surprise us and make us think, "Of course! It really is like that!"

White squirrels live in the town of Olney, Illinois. For a newspaper article about the squirrels, writer Pamela Selbert invented some fresh new similes. She had seen the squirrels only in photographs and wrote that they *"looked to have been carved from ivory or white chocolate."* When she finally saw one of the squirrels, she described it as *"bright as though lit by some inner source."* She wrote that its tail was *"swaying like the train on a wedding gown."*

Ivory . . . white chocolate . . . an inner light . . . a wedding gown . . . to describe *squirrels?* Those are imaginative similes from an imaginative writer!

A second kind of comparison is metaphor. Think of a metaphor as **an equals sign (=).** You make a metaphor when you say **something *is* something else,** such as:

"You **are** a breath of fresh air."
"This job **is** a chain around my neck."

The Bible is full of similes and metaphors. Here are a few examples:

Simile	Metaphor
"All we **like sheep** have gone astray." (Isaiah 53:6, KJV)	**"The Lord is my shepherd."** (Psalm 23:1)
"Therefore everyone who hears these words of mine and puts them into practice is **like a wise man who built his house on the rock** . . .But everyone who hears these words of mine and does not put them into practice is **like a foolish man who built his house on sand.**" (Matt. 7:24, 26)	"Watch out for false prophets. They come to you in sheep's clothing, but inwardly **they are ferocious wolves.**" (Matt. 7:15)
	"I am the vine; you are the branches." (John 15:5)

Simile and metaphor are powerful tools for a writer. In only a few words, they draw an instant picture for the reader. They help you explain difficult ideas because they compare something hard with something simple. Whether you use a simile or a metaphor, **keep it clear.** If you write, "Alfred was like an old sock," your reader will ask *"How* was Alfred like an old sock?" Explain your comparison, or your meaning will be lost. At the same time, **a little mystery keeps your reader curious.** The parables of Jesus are metaphors and similes, and most of the time Jesus did not explain them in detail, but left his hearers to figure out his meaning.

Start-Up:

Write down some similes and metaphors which you have heard people use.

Look around the place where you are right now. Describe different things, or describe how you feel, using **two similes and two metaphors which you make up yourself.**

Intermediate:

For each of the following overused similes or metaphors, **write a fresh one to replace it.** First identify each statement as a metaphor or a simile. Then think carefully about the meaning of each one. If the original is a simile, write a new simile. If it's a metaphor, write a new metaphor.

"The news hit me like a ton of bricks."
"My friend is the Rock of Gibraltar."
"I feel like a million bucks today."
"He went through here like a tornado."

Think of four other tired, overused similes or metaphors. Write new ones to express the same ideas.

Advanced:

Read Jesus' parable of the prodigal son in Luke 15:11-32. Like most of Jesus' parables, it's an **extended metaphor** (a metaphor carried out into a story). **Write your own parable** as an **extended metaphor** which expresses the same truths as the prodigal son parable.

D2 Lively Language

Megawatt Writing

This lesson will help you "turn up the volume" of your writing to emphasize important points.

Is it possible to write a dull story about a trip to outer space? Read this:

I went to the planet Neptune. It was fun. I saw lots of interesting things. Neptune is a funny color. I only got scared once. That was when some Neptunites chased me. People who live on Neptune are called Neptunites. I got away. Then I flew home.

Ho-hum. **That's low-watt writing.** Sometimes writers write in a dull style on purpose: for humor, to portray a dull character, or (as we did here) to illustrate "blah" writing. Normally you want to grab your reader's interest with writing that sparkles. Occasionally you want **extreme strength and force.** You want **intensity**. You want to do **megawatt writing**.

Some writers add *intensity* to their writing the EASY WAY! They WRITE in ALL CAPITALS. They use *italics* and underlining and even *both at once.* Do you know WHAT ELSE??? They never *ever* forget those handy EXCLAMATION POINTS!!!

Yes, we use **bold** and *italics* in this curriculum to emphasize certain points; but too much is like being around someone who SHOUTS all the time. You soon learn to ignore it.

When do you need megawatt writing?
  • when you want to stir your reader's emotions (feelings)
  • when you fear the reader will miss something important
  • when you need to overcome the reader's resistance to your ideas

Here are four solid ways to take your writing from weak to megawatt:

1. Show the emotion.
   Weak: She looked at her test grade and felt bad.
   Megawatt: As soon as she saw her test grade, she shut her eyes tight and mashed the paper into a wad while hot tears escaped down her cheeks.

2. Be definite rather than vague.
   Weak: Our family is happy about Dad's new job.
   Megawatt: At last Dad is going to be a park ranger! We kids fixed him a celebration dinner last night. Even when I burned the pork chops, everybody just laughed.

3. Fill in details.
   Weak: I went to camp and had a really, really good time.
   Megawatt: Every morning at Camp Wood Tick, we jumped into the cold lake for a swim. That woke us up! Then we stuffed ourselves with gooey pancakes and hiked in the woods, which smelled like Christmas. Later we worked up a sweat with games on a dusty field. One afternoon we did wood carving, and I carved my name from a single piece of yellowish maple. I'm definitely going back to Camp Wood Tick next summer!

4. Use fewer words at times. In 1, 2, and 3 we added to the writing. Sometimes you increase intensity if you get rid of extra words instead. Shorter sentences have more punch.
    Weak: Excuse me, there is an approaching hazard which you may want to avoid.
    Megawatt: Look out for that bus!

Start-Up:

Go back to the Neptune story at the start of this lesson. On scratch paper, **rewrite that very low-watt story into a megawatt story.** Use the **four methods above:** show the emotion, be definite, fill in details, and use some (not all) short sentences.
Before you write, answer these questions for yourself: How did I feel about landing on Neptune? What did I see? What color was the ground? the sky? What happened just before the Neptunites showed up? Did they seem friendly at first? How did I get away? How did I feel when I took off and left Neptune?

Intermediate:

All your life you have wanted to be an advertising writer and write TV and radio commercials or magazine and newspaper ads. At last you have a job interview with the Whammo Laundry Soap Company. The big boss hands you a piece of paper and growls, "We just fired our ad writer. Here's the last TV commercial he wrote. **Let's see you rewrite it.** Remember, you have to convince everybody to buy Whammo Soap!"

You take a look at the ad, and you see why they fired their other ad writer. Here's the script for the commercial:

> "Whammo Laundry Soap gets things clean. Maybe you should try it. Some people don't like it, but you probably will. It doesn't cost a lot, at least not as much as some other soaps. So when you get around to it, go to the store and get our soap."

Take out your stack of scratch paper (which of course you brought with you) and go to work. Make notes based on the **four methods above:** show the emotion, be definite, fill in details, and use some (not all) short sentences. In addition, write some answers to these questions:

- What emotions do I want listeners to feel?
- Why might people tune out this ad? How can I be sure to get their attention?
- How can I make sure people hear and remember the name of the soap?
- What are some weak or unconvincing words in the script? What stronger and more convincing words can I substitute?

Now **rewrite the commercial in megawatt style.** Good luck! We hope you get the job!

Advanced:

Go back to the Neptune story at the start of this lesson. Rewrite that very low-watt story into **a megawatt story of at least a full page.** Use the four methods above, but keep in mind that you don't want every sentence to shout at your reader. **Vary your tone** so you keep some parts of the story quiet, then surprise your reader with a burst of intensity.

D3 Lively Language

Understatement

This lesson will help you use the power of saying less than you could say in your writing.

For almost 20 years we lived on Lake Superior. Winter there is cold, dark and long. People will come in from a snowstorm, coated with snow, faces red with cold, eyes streaming tears from the wind. If you ask "What's it like out there?" they will answer, **"Not too bad."**

"Not too bad." **That is an understatement.** To understate is **to say less than you could say, or to say it less strongly.** If you see a picture of the current home run king and you say "He's a pretty good hitter," you have made an understatement. When you understate in your writing, you **hold back your natural emotions and make things "smaller" than they are.**

The opposite of understatement is **exaggeration**. To exaggerate is to make something "bigger" than it is. "I kicked that ball a mile!" "I'm going to get grounded for the rest of my life!"

Here are some examples of exaggeration, ordinary statement, and understatement:

Exaggeration	Ordinary Statement	Understatement
Turn up the heat! I'm about to freeze to death!	It's cold in here.	It's not as warm in here as it could be.
This box weighs a ton.	This box is heavy.	I may need a little help lifting this box.
Everybody in the universe knows who I am.	I am famous.	You might have heard of me.
It sounded like a meteorite crashed into the back yard!	That was a loud noise.	Did you hear something?

Understatement helps you accomplish several things in your writing:

1. Humor. Understatement can be funny in a quiet way. You don't laugh out loud, but you smile a little. In the opening sentence from my *Jackpine Point Adventure #2, Ice Festival,* narrator David Malloy says:

> When the snowball hit me between my collar and my right ear and half of it slid between my sweatshirt and me, I knew this wasn't the most fun day of my life.

David could have said "this was a terrible day" or "this was a rotten day." Instead he says, "this wasn't the most fun day of my life." **That's an understatement.**

2. Attention. Understatement is like a loud whisper. It makes the reader go back and ask, *"What* was that again?" At the beginning of *Stuart Little,* E.B. White uses the whisper of understatement to grab our attention:

When Mrs. Frederick C. Little's second son was born, everybody noticed
that he was not much bigger than a mouse. The truth of the matter was,
the baby looked very much like a mouse in every way.

If your baby brother turned out to be a mouse, you would be shocked, amazed, even terrified. "Everybody noticed" is **an understatement.** Two pages later the book says:

The doctor was delighted with Stuart and said that it was very unusual
for an American family to have a mouse.

"Very unusual"—**that is an understatement!**

3. Modesty. A good writer does not have to give every detail about everything. You can tone down embarrassing or unpleasant descriptions with **understatement.**

Start-Up:

Read each statement under "Exaggeration" and "Ordinary Statement." On scratch paper, **complete the chart by writing an "Understatement" for each.**

Exaggeration	Ordinary Statement
I'm starving!	I'm hungry.
You are the kindest, most generous person in the history of the whole world.	You are kind and generous.
My goldfish is the ugliest fish that ever swam in water.	My goldfish is ugly.
When Uncle Will, Aunt Amelia and my cousins arrived at our front door, it was like a combination army and traveling circus had showed up.	Uncle Will, Aunt Amelia and my cousins made a lively and noisy arrival at our house.

Intermediate:

The following paragraph is written in an exaggerated style. **Rewrite it to make it a good example of understatement.** You probably agree with the exaggeration, so it won't be easy.

We writers are the most imaginative and creative people on planet earth. We are as brilliant as a streak of lightning which flashes across the night sky. Writers are so smart, the government should call on us to solve all problems. If we writers ran things, the world would be an almost perfect place. The only thing which would not be perfect is that some people in the world would not be writers.

Advanced:

Choose a subject about which people tend to write in an excited, emotional and even exaggerated way, such as sports, war, love, faith, or politics. On scratch paper, write a page or so about that subject **in an understated style.** Not every sentence has to be an understatement, but the overall tone should be understated.

D4 Lively Language

In Other Words

This lesson will help you express an idea without using its name.

You've walked miles down a dusty road on a hot day. The road crosses a stream. You notice the water is a strange reddish color, but you're so thirsty you don't care. You rush down to the stream, and just as you're about to take a big gulp of water, you see a sign: "WATER UNSAFE! DO NOT DRINK!" If that sign had gone on and on about streams and woods and fish and nature, you would have been poisoned before you had time to read it.

Sometimes simple and direct statements are best—but not always. Anybody can write "I was tired." Suppose instead you write this:

> "I fought to keep my eyes open. I yawned so big, my jaw hurt. People around me talked on and on about something and I nodded but I didn't understand. With stinging eyes I stared at a couch across the room. A big cozy pillow lay at one end of it. All I wanted was to fall onto that couch, curl up with that pillow and go to sleep."

ZZZZzzzzz . . . oh, sorry. You communicated! We not only *know* you're tired, we *feel* it. But notice, **the word *tired* never appears in that paragraph!** You said it without saying it.

Since there is no special word for this skill, we'll call it the ability to write **"in other words."** It means **you can convince your reader of an idea without using its name.**

In Jack London's short story "To Build A Fire," a man hikes along a frozen creek in the Yukon in sub-zero weather. Only a dog is with him. A muzzle of frost has built up around the man's beard. He has been warned not to travel alone, but he is sure that by 6 p.m. he can reach a camp where there are other people.

Read this excerpt from "To Build A Fire." **As you read, notice how you feel:**

> He unbuttoned his jacket and shirt and drew forth his lunch. The action consumed no more than a quarter of a minute, yet in that brief moment the numbness laid hold of the exposed fingers. He did not put the mitten on, but, instead, struck the fingers a dozen sharp smashes against his leg. Then he sat down on a snow-covered log to eat. The sting that followed upon the striking of his fingers against his leg ceased so quickly that he was startled, he had had no chance to take a bite of biscuit. He struck the fingers repeatedly and returned them to the mitten, baring the other hand for the purpose of eating. He tried to take a mouthful, but the ice-muzzle prevented. He had forgotten to build a fire and thaw out. He chuckled at his foolishness, and as he chuckled he noted the numbness creeping into the exposed fingers.

When you read that, how do you feel? *C-c-c-cold!* But in that passage the author **never uses the word "cold!"** Instead he *shows* us how the cold affects the man's body and mind. The author understands the experience of cold so well that he convinces us without using the word.

Start-Up:

Think of traveling alone through a desert at the hottest part of the day. You have drunk the last of your water and you are miles from any place you hope to find other people. On scratch paper **make a lot of notes about your imagined experience:**

How does the heat affect you?
How do your eyes feel?
How do your feet feel?
How does your tongue feel?
Is your thinking clear? Confused?
What are you looking for?
What do you hear?
What are you thinking about?
What do you wish?
What are your worries?

On scratch paper, **write a story of at least four sentences** to give the idea of the desert heat. Borrow freely from your notes, but **do NOT use the words,** *heat, hot, warm* or *warmth.*

Intermediate:

When you read the excerpt from "To Build A Fire," you probably felt something else besides cold: a mounting sense of danger. Throughout the story Jack London gradually builds a sensation of fear, even as the man keeps telling himself he will make it.

Do the same exercise as in *Start-Up,* with two differences:

• Make your story about as long as the excerpt from "To Build A Fire."
• Try to express a sense of growing fear as well as a sense of heat.

In your story, do not use the words, *heat, hot, warm* or *warmth,* and do not use the words *fear, frightened* or *afraid.*

Advanced:

Read the instructions for *Start-Up* and *Intermediate* but don't do the exercises.

Any writer can try to imagine hiking alone through cold or heat, but the writing will be truer if the writer has actually gone through the experience. Think of an experience of your own in which you felt a particular way: tired, proud, humble, jealous, trusting, nervous, joyful, angry . . . you get the idea. **Write a story approximately the length of the excerpt from "To Build A Fire," expressing that idea without using the word or any form of the word.** The type of questions we provide under *Start-Up* will help stir your thinking.

E1 Special Features

Get a Grip (Titles)

This lesson will help you create strong titles for your writings.

"I make lists of titles. Is that weird?"

My young friend was worried. Every time a good title came to her mind, she wrote it down, even if she did not have a story to go with it.

If she's weird, then so am I, because **I keep a title list.** When I hear or think of anything that would make a good title, I write it down and keep it in a **"Title" file.**

Apparently I was very young when I started the title habit. Recently my husband Dale and I moved into the house where I grew up. As we cleaned out closets, we found a list of titles in my little-kid handwriting. The list was titled "Titles."

Titles are vital! When you put a title on a piece of your work, **you give that work a name.** A person's name is sometimes called a "handle." Have you ever tried to pick up a suitcase with no handle? It's very awkward.

A good title is like the handle on a suitcase. It gives you and your reader a **solid grip** on your story, article, poem or whatever you write. Nobody talks about "that book about the spider." Everybody talks about *"Charlotte's Web."*

The right title can come to you *before, during,* or *after* you write your piece.

Before: **You may get a good title, add it to your title list, and then later—maybe years later—write a piece to go with it.** One day this phrase came into my head: "See You Later, Ellie Vader." I had no idea what it meant (I still don't) but I liked the sound of it. I played around with it and changed it to "See You Later, Elevator." Later I wrote a play by that title.

During: **You may think of a title halfway through a piece. Then you may change your mind, maybe several times.** I had particular trouble with the title of one play. At different times during the writing I called it "Beneath That Flood," "At the Corner of Walk and Don't Walk" and several other names I've forgotten. By the time I finished the play, the title was "In Search of Antlers."

After: **You may even write the entire work and still not have a title, at least not a good one.** Another of my plays was originally titled "Blue Engine." Years later, when the play was about to finally appear on stage, I knew I had to change the title to "Blue Engine Blues."

Some writers think it's smart to title their works "Untitled." That's like calling a person "Hey You" instead of using the person's name. My college English teacher insisted that everything we wrote had to have a title. She said people who use "Untitled" are just too lazy to think of a title!

A title can raise questions and make the reader curious. Good examples are the titles of Harry Kemelman's "rabbi" mysteries, such as *Friday the Rabbi Slept Late* and *Saturday the Rabbi Went Hungry*.

A title can simply tell what the work is about. Marguerite Henry titled most of her animal stories by the name of the main character: *Misty of Chincoteague, Black Gold, Brighty of the Grand Canyon, Cinnabar the One O'Clock Fox*.

A title should be easy to understand when you say it out loud. Dale and I wrote a book on ecology which the publisher titled *While Creation Waits*. When people hear the title, they think it's *Wild Creation Waits*. (The publisher—not the writer—has the final say about the title!)

I still keep a title list. Here are some I have not used, where I got them, and why I like them:

Last Chance for Cherries   A road sign in Michigan. I like this for the repeated ch sound in chance and cherries, and for the questions it raises.
Anvil Wanted   A newspaper ad. It raised questions in my mind.
No Harm to Dolphins   From a tuna can. I liked the sound of the words together.
The Five Basic Grandkids   Someone told me he would spend Christmas with his grandmother. When I asked who would be there, he said "the five basic grandkids." I loved it! If I used this title, I might change it to "The Eight Basic Grandkids" to repeat the long ay sound in "eight" and "basic."
American Gold   It's a phrase from a folk song. Again, I just liked the sound of it.
Daphne the Duck is Dead   A friend said this. Nothing mysterious—he was talking about his family's pet duck. It's actually sad, but it *sounds* funny.

Start-Up:

Make up at least five titles. No, you don't have to write stories to go with them. Just make up five titles. Use them to **start your own "Title List."** Keep the list somewhere you can easily find it. Plan to add to your list any time you think of a good title.

Intermediate:

Look through your own bookshelves and your own memory. **Find titles** you think are especially effective and write them down. **For each title, try to answer these questions:**
    1. Why does this title strike you as a good "handle" for this work?
    2. Why do you think the author chose this title? (We're asking you to speculate about a writer's mind—always hazardous! Still it's interesting to try to figure out the reasons.)
Then start your own title list as instructed in *Start-Up*.

Advanced:

Do everything under *Intermediate*, with this addition: No doubt you have already written a great deal and have titled many of your own works. **Take three works you have written, evaluate their titles, and write two new titles for each.** One title should raise questions, and one should simply express what the work is about (if your titles don't already do that). Be sure your titles are easy to understand when you read them aloud.

E2 Special Features

Opening Hook

This lesson will help you grab and hold your reader's attention.

"Marley was dead, to begin with."

With that news, Charles Dickens begins his book *A Christmas Carol*. Most of *A Christmas Carol* is written in a more complex style, but Dickens gets his story rolling with one short catchy sentence. It's interesting. It's mysterious. **It makes the reader want to keep reading.**

"Marley was dead, to begin with" is an **opening hook**. Dickens "hooks" us and pulls us into his story. **The hook raises questions which we hope the story will answer:** Who was Marley? Why doesn't the writer seem more upset by his death? If his death is only the start of the story, then the story must be about someone else, but who? Most important—what happens next?

Here are some other examples of strong opening hooks from both fiction and non-fiction works. As you read them, notice the questions they raise in your mind.

I did it—I should have known better. —Saki (H.H. Munro), "Reginald"

"Where's Papa going with that ax?" said Fern to her mother as they were setting the table for breakfast. —E.B. White, *Charlotte's Web*

For the first fifteen years of our lives, Danny and I lived within five blocks of each other and neither of us knew of the other's existence. —Chaim Potok, *The Chosen*

When the motorcycle cop came roaring up, unexpectedly, out of Never-Never Land (the way motorcycle cops do), the man was on his hands and knees in the long grass beside the road, barking like a dog. —James Thurber, "The Topaz Cufflinks Mystery"

For students of bird life, owls are the last frontier.
—Julio de la Torre, *Owls*

Once in a while you find yourself in an odd situation.
—Thor Heyerdahl, *Kon-Tiki*

True!—nervous—very, very dreadfully nervous I had been and am; but why *will* you say that I am mad? —Edgar Allan Poe, "The Tell-Tale Heart"

Bill Biggart walked two miles from his apartment near Union Square to reach Ground Zero on the morning of the attack, taking pictures along the way, and he went about 100 feet too far.
— Jerry Adler, "Shooting To The End," *Newsweek*

If you have never visited the British Museum, now is the time to go.
—Kathleen Ritmeyer, "The Rebirth of the British Museum," *Biblical Archaeology Review*

Start-Up:

Gather a bunch of books and magazines. Read the first sentence of each book. (Skip over any introductory material and start with the main part of the book.) Read the first sentences of articles in the magazines. **Find some strong "opening hooks" which you especially like. Copy them onto scratch paper. Then write down the questions they raise in your mind.** Keep your notes as good examples for your own writing.

Note: Questions raised by the opening hook do not have to be answered in the first paragraph. The reader may not learn the answers until the end of the book or article.

Intermediate:

First follow the *Start-Up* instructions.

Next, read the following paragraph. It's the opening of the playwright Moss Hart's autobiography *Act One*. As the story begins, he is a 12-year-old New York boy who is fascinated by the theatre. That afternoon, though he does not yet know it, he will see Broadway for the first time. **But we have cheated: we have replaced Hart's opening hook with a different, weaker sentence. Write your own opening hook for this story.** (Moss Hart's opening hook is in the Teacher's Guide section. Hint: it is rather simple.)

> The music store was a dirty gray building in New York City. It was just around the corner from where we lived, and I worked there every afternoon from three o'clock until seven, while its owner, a violin and piano teacher on the side, gave the lessons which more or less supported the store. There was apparently no great passion for music in the Bronx at that time, and the sparseness of the customers, other than Mr. Levenson's pupils themselves, allowed me to finish my homework as rapidly as possible and then pore greedily over as many copies of *Theatre Magazine* as the library would allow me to take out at one time.

Advanced:

First follow the *Start-Up* instructions. You will probably find some first sentences which are *not* good opening hooks: they don't raise questions or make you curious or make you want to keep reading. **Identify at least five of those "dud" openings** and copy them onto other sheets of scratch paper. **Rewrite each one to make it into a better opening hook.** It will take several tries and you will scribble and cross out a lot. That's okay. That's how a real writer works, and you *are* a real writer.

E3 Special Features

Whose Point of View?

This lesson will help you discover different viewpoints for the same story.

"Through whose eyes shall I tell my story?"

The writer Graham Greene asked himself that question in a journal during a trip to the Congo in Africa. Greene was planning a book to be set in the Congo. When Greene asked "Through whose eyes shall I tell my story?" he was searching for the right **point of view.**

What is **point of view?** A writer usually tells a story in one of two ways:

"**I** did this, **I** went there, **I** saw that . . ."
   (or)
"**They** did this, **she** went there, **he** said that, . . ." (but never "**I** did this . . .")

If the writer uses "I," the story is written in *first person.* **It is told from the** *first person point of view.*

If the writer uses "he, she, they, it, So-and-So," but does not use "I," the story is written in *third person.* **It is told from the** *third person point of view.*

You may never read or write a story which says **"you did this, you went there."** If you did, the story would be **written in** *second person,* **told from the** *second person point of view.* You're right, **this curriculum is written in second person!** Second person is most often used in curriculum, advertisements, and advice articles ("You can be a faster sprinter if you take off your hiking boots and wear track shoes").

Let's take a closer look at the first person and third person points of view.

First Person: In a story told in *first person,* the **"I"** character is called the **narrator.** The narrator can be the author or a made-up character. *Black Beauty* is written in first person, but the narrator is not the author Anna Sewell; it's the horse Black Beauty.

First person brings your reader inside the narrator's head. The reader sees everything through the narrator's eyes. If your narrator is not interesting, the story is not interesting either. You can't bring the reader into any other characters' heads—unless your narrator is a mind-reader!

The narrator is not always the main character. For example, the Sherlock Holmes stories are written in *first person.* Dr. Watson is the narrator. Watson has no purpose in the stories except to observe and report what Holmes does (and help a little now and then). Many other detective stories are narrated by a friend of the detective, such as Captain Hastings for Hercule Poirot or Archie Goodwin for Nero Wolfe. The "narrator-friend" works especially well for detective stories because the writer can bring the reader close to the action without revealing the workings of the detective's mind.

Third Person: In a story told in *third person,* the writer steps back from the story and uses "he, she, they, it" rather than "I." Third person does not have to be cold and distant. You can still bring your readers inside your characters' heads if you clearly **show the reader how your characters feel and think.** *Charlotte's Web* is written in *third person,* but the reader always knows exactly what Wilbur the pig thinks and feels.

A writer is more free in third person than in first person. In third person you can open up the heads of *several* characters in your story, not just "I." If your story has a lot of characters and you try to bring the reader into *all* their minds, you'll confuse the reader and yourself as well. Decide which one or two characters you will let the reader see into—the ones "through whose eyes" you will tell your story.

Start-Up:

Look through several books, newspaper stories and magazine articles. **Figure out which point of view each of them uses: first person, second person or third person.** On scratch paper write the title of each piece. After the title, write "1" if it's written in first person, "2" if it's written in second person, or "3" if it's written in third person.

Pick out two sentences from your samples. Copy them on scratch paper. **Rewrite them so they are from a different point of view.**

Intermediate:

First do the *Start-Up* activity. Then . . .

If you write in third person and open up *every* head in your story, letting the reader see through *everyone's* eyes, you write from the **omniscient** point of view. You may have heard God described as omniscient. It means "having all knowledge." If your story has more than one or two characters, it's very difficult to write or read a story from the omniscient point of view. Your reader is not God and neither are you!

More useful to the writer is the **third person limited** point of view. You select one or two or maybe three minds to open up for your readers. They may or may not be your main characters, but they are the ones whose perspective you will use to tell the story. Your story will change depending on whose eyes you let the reader see through.

Pick a scene from one of your favorite books or short stories which is written from the **third person limited** point of view. Identify whose perspective is shown. **Rewrite the scene so it is still third person limited, but it opens up a different character's head.**

Advanced:

Do the *Intermediate* activity (which includes doing the *Start-Up* activity). However, for *Intermediate,* **rewrite the "third person limited" scene from the perspective of an object nearby,** as though the object can think and can understand what is going on.

E4 Special Features

Let's Talk (Dialogue)

This lesson will help you put believable words in the mouths of your characters.

When you write a story, you naturally find yourself writing *he said* or *she said.* You not only report what people did, you quote their words. You are writing **dialogue.**

Dialogue is simply **conversation in writing.** It's easy to write dialogue. Just put words into your characters' mouths:

"This game is really exciting," Maria said.
"I think we're going to win," Jacob said.
"Our team has never played better," Andrew said.
"I agree," Kristine said.

Did you fall asleep? That dialogue is correct, but it has no life. It doesn't sound real. **The speakers all sound alike.** You could swap the names around and it would make no difference. In real life, **different people say things differently.** You don't always say things the way your parents or neighbors would say them. You and your friends don't talk exactly alike.

Listen! The **key to writing good dialogue** is not your pencil or your keyboard, but your **ears. Listen when people talk. Listen to how different people talk differently.**

When you write dialogue, **let your individual characters speak individually.**

Here are examples of ways your characters can speak as individuals. To help yourself hear the difference, **say the example quotes out loud:**

1. Vocabulary (Formal or informal? Does the character use "big" or "little" words?)

"I fear that I shall be overdue for my appointment."

"I'm afraid I'm going to arrive late."

"Yikes! I'm never gonna make it!"

2. Sentence length (Does the character speak long thoughts? Or short and choppy?)

"Does she honestly think I would ever say anything like she says I said when I have never in my life said anything at all like that?"

"Does she honestly think I would say that? When I have never said anything like that in my life?"

"She thinks I said that? Honest? How? I've never said anything like that. Never in my life. Ever."

3. Correctness or incorrectness (Does the character sound educated? Uneducated? Uneducated, but trying to fake it?)

"We have no fear of those lawless ones."

"We aren't scared of those criminals."

"We ain't a-feared o' them crooks."

4. Forcefulness (Is the character decisive? Uncertain? Wishy-washy?)

"At the next intersection I am going to turn right."

"Well, I guess maybe at the next intersection I should turn right."

"Uh, should I maybe turn at the next intersection? Left or right, or what?"

Here's an example of how dialogue can show differences between characters.
In *Brighty of the Grand Canyon*, President Theodore Roosevelt dedicates the first footbridge over the Colorado River. The old canyon man "Uncle Jim" Owen argues that the burro Brighty should be first to cross the bridge. He reminds the crowd that a donkey carried Jesus into Jerusalem. Author Marguerite Henry was not there, but she invented **convincing dialogue:**

"And mind ye, fellers!" Uncle Jim shook his big-knuckled forefinger. "Ever since that day, burros has been marked with the cross. Look-a-here!" He traced the black stripe down Brighty's back and the crossbar over his shoulder. "See them lines? Where'd ye find a stouter-marked cross than this 'un?"

Teddy Roosevelt replies:

"Yes, gentlemen, Brighty has earned the emblem he wears. He has borne burdens and blazed trails. He has packed the sand and cement that built the very bulwark of the bridge. What could be more fitting than that these two frontiersmen, James Owen and Bright Angel, dedicate the new bridge?"

Jim Owen and Teddy Roosevelt are both rugged men of the outdoors, but their speech could not be more different. **We know who they are from how they talk.** They are **individuals who speak individually.**

Start-Up:

Keep pencil and scratch paper handy. As much as possible today (or tomorrow if it's already late in the day), **write down things you hear people say.** Write what is said as exactly as you can, and note who said it. If the person emphasizes particular words, underline them. The talkers should be people you know; no TV or radio programs. Of course you can't write down everything you hear, but **fill three or four sheets of paper.**

Now pick out one of the quotes. Imagine someone else saying it. **Rewrite the quote so it sounds more like that other person.** (It will help if you **say the quotes out loud.**)

Intermediate:

Do the *Start-Up* activity, but choose at least **four quotes** to rewrite.

Advanced:

Do the first paragraph of *Start-Up*. **Invent at least three characters** who are very different from the people who actually said the quotes you wrote down. Using as many of your quotes as possible, **rewrite the quotes into a dialogue for your imagined characters.**

F1 Even Better

The Minus Sign (Cutting)

This lesson will help you cut out unneeded words.

• Christmas trees do not naturally grow in Christmas-tree shape. As they grow, long branches are **cut off** so the trees grow thick and dense.

• The flowers in our front yard bloomed like crazy for the first part of the summer. Then they quit. **"Cut them back,"** a friend told me. Feeling like a murderer, I took scissors and cut off the tops of the plants. They bloomed again and kept blooming until frost.

• The pine tree in our back yard dates back to the Civilian Conservation Corps of the 1930s. It's a handsome tree, but it had a lot of dead and broken branches. We **cut out** the dead wood. Our pine now looks as though it will last another 70 years.

• Jesus spoke of the fruitful grapevine which must be pruned (**cut back**). If the gardener prunes the vine, it will produce even more fruit. (John 15:2)

Christmas trees, flowers, pine trees and grapevines are all improved if they are cut back. **You can often improve your writing if you cut it back.**

Cutting hurts a writer's pride, but a mature writer goes ahead and cuts, if cutting is the best way to fix a problem. Here are several **tools you can use to make cuts:**

Delete key: If you write with a computer, you can delete unwanted words and they disappear. But what if you decide you want them back? Give your words a second chance. Print out your work and cross things out with a pencil, and do it so you can still read the words.

Pen: If you write with a pen or pencil, make your cuts by crossing out, but do it so you can still read your words, in case you decide to put something back. Cross out with a different color ink so you can quickly see what and how much you have cut.

Scissors and tape: If you decide to cut out big chunks, take scissors and actually cut the paper and tape it back together. Your paper will look funny, but you can recopy it later.

When you cut, start with the idea that **every word should have a job.** Are all your words busy working for you? Remove anything which does not help you say what you want to say. Decide what matters, and cut what does not matter. **You are always smart to cut these extras:**

1. **Side trips.** Where does your story leave its main path and wander off into unnecessary descriptions or opinions?
2. **Road blocks.** What gets in the way of the reader's understanding? Are there confusing ideas which take too much time and space to explain?
3. **Dull stuff.** When you read your work, where do *you* lose interest? Your reader will lose interest there too (if not sooner).
4. **Showing off.** Have you written something simply to show off your knowledge or to be funny, even though it does not help you accomplish your purpose? Cut it out!

Start-Up:

Copy the following paragraph onto scratch paper, or type it into your computer and print it. **Cross out anything you think should be cut.** If you decide to keep that part after all, make a mark to remind yourself—perhaps circle the words or put a check mark beside them. Then **rewrite the paragraph as you want it.** You can **re-arrange ideas** if you like.

> When my cousin Amanda won the spelling bee, I think maybe I was almost as proud as she was. Some cousins aren't very close. She had a huge smile when she accepted her prize. My face hurt because I was smiling so much too. My face also hurt when I got frostbite. I'm a good speller, but Amanda is even better. My friend Kyle is not close to his cousins.

Intermediate:

Follow the same instructions as *Start-Up*, but use this paragraph:

> The Ferris wheel shook and our cage began to rise backwards. I leaned forward a little. It's like in a car when you put on the brakes. Up we went through the evening air as though carried on the toodly notes of the carnival music. Once I went up in a skyscraper and I couldn't look down. I almost fell out of my neighbor's treehouse. James talked me into this ride. I looked down at the carnival lights. A streak of orange sunset stayed on the horizon. When we reached the top, the wheel stopped. I held my breath, which I can do for about two and a half minutes. James began to rock the cage. I felt sick. Last winter I got the flu.

Advanced:

Do you want to feel like a serious working writer? Here is a taste of professional writer pain. **Sometimes a writer must make cuts simply because the work is too long.** We often have to write to fit a specified space: this many pages, this many inches, this many words. If it hurts to cut your bad writing, it hurts worse to cut your *good* writing just because it won't fit!

In this excerpt from my *Jackpine Point Adventure* #4, *The Dark Lighthouse*, David Malloy approaches the ruined lighthouse tower. This is about 130 words long. Copy it onto scratch paper. **Then cut it to about 65 words.** If it's easier, go by the number of lines instead of the number of words. (No fair just cutting off the bottom half!) **Re-arrange ideas** if you want.

> The tower was deserted. I kicked at one of the red-and-white chunks lying around, pieces of the tower that had crumbled off. The red was the brick, the white was the plaster. Around the tower was a screen of chopped-off jackpine stumps and younger saplings. Every now and then somebody tried to cut it all back, but the stuff kept growing up again. I pushed through the scratchy brush to the door.
>
> Or rather the doorway. There was no door, only a rough opening with a slab of cement where the top of the door frame should be.
>
> I stepped inside onto broken chunks of stuff. I was in a tall brick tube. A bird shot out through a window which was only a hole full of light and sapling shapes.

F2 Even Better

The Plus Sign (Expanding)

This lesson will help you fill in communication gaps in your writing.

A couple of years ago we enclosed a newsy form letter with our Christmas cards. Some friends wrote back, "Thanks for the card, but why didn't you tell us any of your news?" We must have accidentally left the form letter out of their card.

No matter what you write, **make sure your readers get "all the news."** In Lesson F1 "The Minus Sign (Cutting)" we talked about how to get rid of extra material. In this lesson we concentrate on **how to add missing material.**

We writers carry so many words and pictures in our heads, we assume our readers see what we see and hear what we hear. They don't, unless we show them.

Here's where it helps to have someone else read what you have written—someone who is on your side but honest. Anyplace that person says "Huh??" you need to explain things more fully. Yes, it's hard when your reader says "Huh??" I usually get frustrated and ask, "How could you possibly *not* understand what I meant?" When I calm down, I can see the holes in my work.

You can't give your reader every detail. You have to choose *where* to expand your work. Ask yourself: **What else does my reader need to know about:**

- **Who?** (Characters: Does your reader *know them* well enough?)
- **What?** (Plot: Can the reader understand the *basic problem* of the story?)
- **Where?** (Setting, place: Have you described the *place* in enough detail?)
- **When?** (Setting, time: Can the reader tell *when* this happened?)
- **Why?** (Motives: Do the people in the story show *reasons* for what they do?)
- **How?** (Actions: Can the reader *keep track* of what is going on?)

Here are some examples of statements with holes which need to be filled in:

"The weather was terrible." What does that mean? If I have planned an outdoor fair, it could mean cold rain. If I have just planted wheat, it could mean scorching sun. If I am in a sailboat race, it could mean no wind. If I plan to travel, it could mean heavy snow. If I want to ski, it could mean no snow. *Show* how the terrible weather *affects* your characters and your story.

"Our dining room is small." Does that mean it's cozy? Too crowded? We're too poor to afford a big enough house? What *effect* does the small dining room have on us and on others?

"He walked slowly into the room." Why slowly? Is he afraid? injured? embarrassed? making a dramatic entrance? shy? What's in the room and why is he entering it? Would he rather not?

Start-Up:

For each of these sentences, make notes about **what else a reader would need to know.** (Hint: What else do *you* want to know? What feels "missing" as you read?) **Make up some details** for each sentence. **Rewrite each sentence** to include those details.

1. Here comes that guy with the lawn mower again.

2. I think this game is going to be exactly like the last game.

3. Martina noticed that Karl's hair looked different.

4. It looks like it's going to snow a lot.

5. My fingernails have gotten really long.

Intermediate:

Here is a bare-bones story. **Make notes of further details** you think a reader should know. From your own imagination, **fill in the missing details. Rewrite the paragraph in expanded form.**

Candace was sorry she had ever thought of going back down into the basement. The box was open now. She lifted out the torn coat and felt bad. She wanted to return what she had found in the pocket, but now she couldn't. Then she heard that sound again. She knew exactly what it meant.

Advanced:

Write a bare-bones story of four or five sentences, similar to the story under *Intermediate*. Consider the **missing parts** which you could fill in. **Choose which details** to supply, and **rewrite the story in expanded form.**

F3 Even Better
I Can Fix That For You

This lesson will help you practice various skills you have learned throughout *Igniting Your Writing!*

Are you ready? You're about to rewrite another writer's published work! You're going to **revise** another writer's writing. (In this book you've often seen the word **rewrite**. **Revise** and **rewrite** mean the same thing. You **do a revision** or **do a rewrite**—same thing.)

Don't panic! We won't ask you to take a famous book off the shelf and rewrite the whole work. You will start much smaller than that.

Actually you will not *start* in this lesson. All through *Igniting Your Writing!* we have asked you to rewrite sample sentences and paragraphs. Sometimes they were from my work; sometimes they were from other books and magazines. In those rewrites you concentrated on one particular skill.

Now you're going to revise a piece of published work, using all or most of the skills you have learned and practiced throughout *Igniting Your Writing!*

What will you revise this time? It's up to you. You, or you and your teacher together, will choose a piece. That's why this lesson does not have *Start-Up*, *Intermediate*, and *Advanced* headings. The level will be set by the difficulty of the piece you choose to rewrite.

You can pick almost anything you find in print, but **it should not be written by a well-known writer. Some possibilities:**

>   short newspaper article   back of a cereal box (if it has a lot of words)
>   letter to the editor in a newspaper   introduction or preface to a book
>   letter to the editor in a magazine   instructions for how to do something
>   advertising brochure   artist notes from a tape or CD

On the next page you'll find summing-up questions and hints from most of the other lessons in *Igniting Your Writing!* (A few of the lessons served as idea-starters. They are not as helpful for revision, unless you feel you need to generate new ideas for your rewrite.) You can also flip back through this book and look at past lessons and the work you did for them.

When you choose your piece to rewrite, ask yourself these questions about the piece. Write your answers on scratch paper and **let your answers guide you as you rewrite.**

A2 Sentence Stretch Where do you see choppy sentences which could be combined?

A3 Sentence Shrink Do some sentences go on and on forever? How can you break them up?

A4 Word Order How can you change the word order to emphasize different ideas?

B1 Verbs Identify the verbs. Do the verbs help the reader see and feel the action? If not, how can you change them?

B2 Nouns Identify the nouns. Are the nouns definite enough? If not, what other nouns would work better?

B3 Adjectives Identify the adjectives. Are they strong enough? Where can you get rid of some adjectives and substitute better nouns?

B4 Adverbs Identify the adverbs. Would this piece be better off with more adverbs? Fewer adverbs? Different adverbs?

D1 Comparisons Does the writer use similes? metaphors? How good are they? How can you improve them? What comparisons can you add?

D2 Megawatt Writing How does this piece touch the reader's emotions? Is it too emotional now? What would make the work more convincing?

D3 Understatement Is the writing so exaggerated that it's hard to believe? Where could understatement make it stronger?

D4 In Other Words Where could you remove a key word and rewrite that part of the piece without using that word (keeping the same idea)?

E1 Titles If the piece has a title, do you like it? How would you improve it? If it does not have a title, what would you title it and why?

E2 Opening Hook What is the opening hook? Can you think of a better one?

E3 Point of View What is the point of view? What are some other possibilities for point of view? Which one works best for this piece?

E4 Dialogue If the piece contains dialogue, is it believable? If the author quotes real people, you can't rewrite the quotes, but you can choose to cut some. If there is no dialogue, would the addition of dialogue help? Who should speak?

F1 Cutting What words are extras? Where could the piece be helped by cutting?

F2 Expanding Where does this piece need to be expanded? (You may not have the information you need to expand the piece, but if you do, go ahead.)

F4 Even Better

Nobody's Perfect

This lesson will help you revise your own work, not only for this assignment but for everything you write.

After *Igniting Your Writing!* is published, I know I'll find things in it which I wish were different. I have written about 50 published books and Bible study guides and about a dozen plays. Today I can look at every one of them and see things I wish I had done differently.

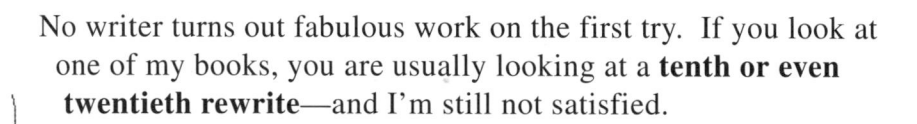

No writer turns out fabulous work on the first try. If you look at one of my books, you are usually looking at a **tenth or even twentieth rewrite**—and I'm still not satisfied.

I enjoy rewriting. I like to see how much better the work can get. But at some point the thing has to go to the printer, and then it's too late to make changes.

You're lucky. **In this lesson you get to rewrite some of your own work,** and you don't have to send it off to a printer tomorrow. You will still be free to rewrite it again later.

Like Lesson F3, this lesson lacks *Start-Up, Intermediate,* and *Advanced* headings. When you take on a rewrite of your own work, it always *feels* like *Advanced!*

Choose a piece of your own writing to revise. It can be something you wrote for a lesson in this book or something else entirely. A good choice would be something you wrote some time ago but have not looked at for a while.

If you have done the *Advanced* level of these lessons, you have already rewritten some of your own pieces. You can choose one of them to rewrite again. (Yes, again!)

As with Lesson F3, on the next page we give you summing-up questions and hints from most of the other lessons in this book. Flip back and look at those lessons too.

Ask yourself the following questions about your piece. Write answers on scratch paper.
It may be harder to answer these questions about your own writing than about someone else's writing. Your answers will still be your best guide as you rewrite.

A2 Sentence Stretch	Where do you have choppy sentences which could be combined?
A3 Sentence Shrink	Do some sentences go on and on forever? How can you break them up?
A4 Word Order	How can the word order be changed to emphasize different ideas?
B1 Verbs	Identify your verbs. Do the verbs help your reader see and feel the action? If not, how can you change them?
B2 Nouns	Identify your nouns. Are the nouns definite enough? If not, what other nouns could you bring in?
B3 Adjectives	Identify your adjectives. Are they strong enough? Should you get rid of some adjectives and substitute better nouns?
B4 Adverbs	Identify your adverbs. Would this piece be better off with more adverbs? Fewer adverbs? Different adverbs?
D1 Comparisons	Did you use similes? metaphors? How good are they? How can you improve them? What comparisons can you add?
D2 Megawatt Writing	How does this piece touch your reader's emotions? How could it be stronger? Or is it too emotional now? Is the reader likely to resist your ideas? What will make the work more convincing?
D3 Understatement	Is the writing so exaggerated that it's hard to believe? Where could understatement make it stronger?
D4 In Other Words	Where can you remove a key word and rewrite that part of the piece without using that word (keeping the same idea)? This may or may not work in this piece, but it would be interesting to try.
E1 Titles	If you gave this piece a title, do you still like it? How would you improve it now? If it does not have a title, what will you title it?
E2 Opening Hook	What opening hook did you use? Can you think of a better one now?
E3 Point of View	What point of view did you use? What are some other possibilities for point of view? Which one would make the work most convincing?
E4 Dialogue	If the piece contains dialogue, is it believable? If you quoted real people, you can't rewrite the quotes, but you can choose to cut some. If there is no dialogue, would the addition of dialogue help? Who should speak?
F1 Cutting	Where does this piece need to be cut?
F2 Expanding	What else does your reader need to know?

Teacher's Guide

General Help

Grading
You have several choices for grading the lessons in *Igniting Your Writing!*

- You can grade on an **absolute scale** based on your judgment of the quality of the student's writing.
- You can grade by **improvement** based on what you already know of the student's writing or based on the first few lessons.
- You can grade on **completion of assignments** if your student struggles to write anything at all. At first, completing an assignment may rate an "A." You may want to give a "B" or "B+" for completion, in order to allow room for the grade to improve.

The "Red Pen" Question
How closely should you correct **technical errors** in grammar, spelling, and punctuation? This question nags at most teachers of writing. Correct usage does matter! Mistakes, especially chronic ones, confuse the reader and undercut the writer's credibility. At the same time, especially with beginning writers, you don't want to be so picky that you cut the heart out of your student's creativity.

The **Problems Chart** on page 82 will help mellow the red-pen problem. Photocopy the Problems Chart and use it to keep a cumulative record of student errors. Make as many copies as you need. Over time, the chart will reveal which mistakes are only **occasional slips** and which mistakes are **consistent problems.** As patterns become clear, you will avoid nagging the student about trivial errors. You can then address the chronic mistakes, one at a time, in separate practice.

Talent Search
While *Igniting Your Writing!* equips young writers with skills for all types of writing, most writers will excel at a particular type (such as persuasion, humor, narrative, technical, essay). The **Strengths Chart** on page 83 will help you identify your young writer's unique skills. Photocopy the Strengths Chart as many times as you need to. Use it to record especially strong features of the student's writing. Over time, the Strengths Chart will reveal **areas where the young writer's work truly shines.** It will help you offer genuine compliments and affirm the writer's gifts. Your young writer may not even be aware of these special abilities until you point out the evidence.

Your First Response

When your student shows you a piece of writing at any stage, **try to make your first comment positive.** Point out some strong feature of the work: it's lively, it's colorful, it makes me curious, I can see it in my mind, it stirs my emotions, it's funny, it makes me feel what you felt (or what the character feels).

Your aim is not to flatter, but **to encourage the student to** *keep writing.* Writers, especially born writers, are often emotionally fragile and melancholy people. The better the writer, the more sensitive he or she may be to criticism. On the other hand, "it's perfect the way it is" is always a lie! Any piece of writing can be improved. More mature writers will want to revise their work to see how much better it can be.

Why Use Scratch Paper?

In *Igniting Your Writing!* we ask students to do most of their work on scratch paper (paper which has been used on one side). We suggest scratch paper for a reason: to emphasize that first drafts (and second and even third drafts) are just that—drafts, attempts, versions. They are not the final product. **Good paper for a first attempt can inhibit the student** because it implies "This has to be perfect on the first try."

Students should do their *final* versions on good paper. Lined or unlined is your choice. If the lesson aim is chiefly to experiment with ideas (such as in Lesson A1 "Word Trade") you can even let the student stay with scratch paper and never do a version on good paper.

Of course you don't *have* to use scratch paper, but why waste good paper on anything but the final version? We are going on the assumption that most households accumulate a lot of paper which is used on one side only. If for some reason scratch paper does *not* pile up in your household, use whatever paper is cheapest and most convenient.

Teacher's Guide for individual lessons follows on pp. 58-81.

Section A
Word Play

These four lessons have a light-hearted tone and a serious purpose: to encourage the young writer to be bold enough to experiment with different ways to use words. If a writer discovers the fun of playing with words, he will try more possibilities and won't quit just because he gets something down on paper. A writer of any age needs willingness and patience to explore alternative ways to express an idea.

Lesson A1 Word Trade

Lesson Aims: To encourage boldness to experiment with words; to promote a more flexible vocabulary.

Watch for: Willingness to try out a variety of words and phrases; imagination and creativity in word choice and combination in the new sentences.

This lesson introduces and explains the term **draft**, which will be new to some students.

Start-Up: This level will work best for "non-writers." Read through the instructions with your student. Let the student talk his way through the sentences. Suggest a couple of verbs (action words) to get started. Have the student write them down; sometimes the act of writing opens up a door to new ideas. If the student is stuck, open a favorite book and search for possible verbs to use. If necessary, suggest words to get the other lists started too.

Intermediate: This level introduces more complexity into the student's writing. It also identifies two examples of **dependent clauses.**

Advanced: This activity will work best for natural writers. Watch out for laziness! A good writer can dash off quick lists of words without much thought. Especially in the longer story, the student may want to lapse back into ordinary dull language. Challenge the student to come up with more imaginative possibilities for word choices. If necessary, the student can write out a sentence from the story and use the same method as for the "Todd" sentence—make alternate lists of possible words.

Lesson A2   Sentence Stretch

Lesson Aims: To smooth out choppy writing; to try various solutions to achieve a smooth flow of words. This lesson pushes the student toward the heart of good writing: *rewriting*.

Watch for: Improvement in the smooth flow of the sentences. Since the ear is an excellent judge of smoothness, the student is instructed to read the new version(s) aloud.

Start-Up: The student is asked to evaluate his work and to rewrite his new sentence(s). Even good writers may resist. You are the best judge of how much to push your young writer. If simply getting words down on paper was a major accomplishment, stop there for now; but keep in mind that *the student will grow as a writer only as he becomes willing to rewrite.*

In the *Start-Up* instructions we tell the student "No fair just putting commas in place of the periods!" Your young writer may try to fix the short sentences by joining them as one sentence with commas for glue (or with no punctuation at all) and no *and's, but's, if's* or *or's* between them. If he does that, he has made a **run-on sentence,** which is an incorrect form. (We define **run-on sentence** for the student in Lesson A3.) Here's an example of how it would be done. **Remember this is incorrect:**

> She threw the egg, she threw it really hard, the egg was raw, it hit my forehead, it went SPLAT! I thought she was my friend, I found out I was wrong.

Intermediate: We ask the student to choose his best effort. Then we ask the student to try to explain *why* that one version works better than the others. Don't insist on a technical answer here. In this case "it sounds better" is perhaps the best answer of all.

Advanced: This level calls for more inventiveness and more discipline. The student must write *original* choppy sentences and then smooth them out. The student is asked to think more deeply about *why* the best version works. Then, just as the student is ready to say "It's good enough," we ask for a rewrite of the "best" version to make it even better.

Lesson A3 Sentence Shrink

Lesson Aims: To practice tightening up overlong sentences; to get a feel for when a sentence is long enough or too long.

Watch for: Awareness of how overlong "rambling" sentences tire out the reader; improvement in the readability and sound of the new, shorter sentences.

Start-Up: Some students will enjoy the long space ship sentence and see nothing wrong with it. Ask them to imagine an entire book written with sentences as long as that one. It would be very difficult to get through. Here is a possible rewrite of the space ship sentence as five shorter sentences. Except for getting rid of a few "and's," we did not change any words:

> (1) You may not believe this, but yesterday a space ship swooped down over my back yard and hovered for a while before it landed. (2) A door opened, a ladder popped out and a Martian with six arms and two heads stood at the doorway. (3) Was I ever scared! (4) When it saw me, it pulled the ladder up and went back inside and took off. (5) By the way, have you looked out your window?

This lesson introduces and explains the term **run-on sentence.** Our rambling space ship sentence is not a run-on sentence. It at least has its punctuation in the right places.

Intermediate: The activity brings home the awkwardness of a rambling sentence by directing the student to make a bad sentence even worse—then to repair it.

Advanced: We introduce the idea that a skillful writer can occasionally break the rules (in this case, write an unusually long sentence) if the writer has a clear purpose and handles the words well.

Lesson A4 Flip It! (Word Order)

Lesson Aim: To understand that a writer can change the emphasis of a sentence by rearranging its words.

Watch for: Willingness to experiment with different word order; awareness of how emphasis changes with different word order.

Start-Up: Here for the first time we give the student permission to play with the words in a published work by a "real" writer! In this case we don't ask the student to improve the work, only to experiment with different emphases he can chieve with different word arrangements. Some of the student's experiments may produce awkward sentences. The student will probably sense that a sentence doesn't sound right, but may need your help to smooth it out.

Intermediate: We give the student the opportunity to do some original writing, then to play around with the order of his own words. This is a non-threatening way to practice rewriting.

Advanced: The paragraph we provide is so convoluted that almost any attempt will improve it. The student should get a clear idea of what ideas he wishes to emphasize before he decides where to change and where to keep the word order.

Section B
Parts of Speech: Part of Writing

Words are the individual bricks from which the writer constructs a piece of work. A writer has various types of words available for various uses. While *Igniting Your Writing!* is not a grammar text, the lessons in this section will help the young writer make effective use of four parts of speech: verbs, nouns, adjectives, and adverbs. **These lessons assume that the student knows basic parts of speech and can identify them in a sentence.** If you are not sure, ask the student to look through a page from any book or magazine and pick out verbs, nouns, adjectives, and adverbs.

Lesson B1   Action! (Verbs)

Lesson Aim: To strengthen the student's writing through the use of vivid verbs which show rather than tell.

Watch for: Imaginative verbs which bring action to life for the reader.

In this lesson we consider verbs **only as action words.** We do not consider the helping verbs such as "am," "is," "are," "can," shall," etc.

Start-Up: We provide the student with sentences containing weak verbs and ask him to substitute stronger verbs. Young writers do not necessarily have huge stores of terrific verbs in their heads. To get ideas, help the student look through some stories by good writers and pick out particularly interesting verbs.

Intermediate: The student must supply original verbs to complete verbless sentences.

Advanced: This activity shows how verbs can set a mood. The student will change the mood of a piece by changing its verbs.

A thesaurus, either in print or on computer, can help a writer choose a better verb or any other part of speech—if the writer uses it sensibly. A thesaurus offers a convenient word list, but the writer must have a sense of which shade of meaning he wants.

Suppose I write, "I need to run out and buy a birthday present." I decide I don't like the verb "run." I go to my thesaurus and look for "run" in the sense of "hurry," and I find these alternatives: sprint, dash, gallop, race, speed, jog.

Obviously I can't just plug any of those verbs into my sentence. I might say "I need to *dash* out" or "I need to *race* out," but "I need to *gallop* out" sounds silly. If I decide to use "*gallop*," I should have a good reason. "*Hurry,*" a perfectly good verb for that sentence, does not even appear in my thesaurus as an alternative to "run." So don't put all your faith in your thesaurus.

Lesson B2 What *Is* This? (Nouns)

Lesson Aim: To guide the student to use more specific and definite nouns.

Watch for: Nouns which are as specific as needed in order to communicate the writer's intention.

Start-Up: For younger students, the concepts of "general" and "specific" may be abstract. The example chart will help make the differences clear. If you're not sure your student gets the concepts, provide a sample noun such as "dog" and ask for a noun which is more general and a noun with is more specific. "Animal" would be a more general noun. A noun for a breed (Dachshund) or a particular dog's name (Spot) would be more specific. "Brown dog" is more specific, but it's not a different noun; it's the same noun with an adjective added.

Intermediate: This level shows that a writer can go overboard with specific nouns. For every noun choice the writer must ask, "How concrete do I have to be *in this case?*" The writer makes most of those choices at an instinctive level—otherwise a page would take months to write—but at times the writer must consciously consider and choose the right level of precision.

Advanced: The student will write about a subject he knows well. Possible topics: the care of an unusual pet, a computer skill, an obscure sport, a hobby which few people practice, a branch of science, a musical instrument, a method of building or repairing something. Your student may insist he possesses no special skills with special terms. Remind him of all the times you have asked him, *"What* do you mean?" or *"What* are you talking about?"

Lesson B3   Tell Us More About It (Adjectives)

Lesson Aim: To encourage the writer to use precise adjectives to focus the meanings of nouns.

Watch for: Adjectives which are fresh and original rather than commonplace.

Start-Up: The struggle of trying to write *without* adjectives shows the writer how common and necessary they are. The writer will be relieved to be able to add adjectives in the rewrite. Notice we ask the writer to make the adjectives as descriptive as possible. Encourage the student to go beyond trite adjectives such as "little," "big," "quiet," or "funny."

Intermediate and *Advanced*: As with verbs in Lesson B1, the student considers how adjectives set a mood in a piece and how changing the adjectives can change the mood.

Here are the *adjectives* in the excerpt from *A Separate Peace*, along with the nouns they modify:

hard thoughts	*sharp* stars	*single, chilled* points . . . *unromantic*	
knife blades	*gentle* occupation	*cold Yankee* stars	*great* love
crowded night skies	*cold* points		

Those adjectives set a tone which is cold, sharp, hard, distant and unfriendly. The phrase "gentle occupation of the snow" seems the exception. In the context of approaching war, the noun "occupation" implies invasion and conquest by an enemy; so even a *gentle* occupation is a threat.

Lesson B4   How Did You Do That? (Adverbs)

Lesson Aim: To thoughtfully use and not overuse adverbs.

Watch for: Understanding of how adverbs help a writer and why their overuse annoys the reader.

For this lesson I searched through my favorite books for examples of adverbs. I was soon frustrated. Powerful nouns, verbs, and adjectives jumped off the pages at me, but I did not often catch my favorite authors using adverbs. My search confirmed that skillful writers are sparing in their use of adverbs. So the next time I *diligently* search my *extremely* large collection of books by *justly* famous authors and fail *miserably* at my *carefully* chosen task . . . Well, it serves me right. *(Rightly?)*

Start-Up: Beginning writers will find enough challenge just coming up with a correct adverb for each blank. Affirm what they have done, then encourage them to search for some colorful and vivid alternatives. Here are several possibilities for sentence #2:

"I can *never* beat you at tennis!" he said *resentfully* as he *furiously* tossed his racket into the air.

"I can *certainly* beat you at tennis!" he said *confidently* as he *carelessly* tossed his racket into the air.

"I can *finally* beat you at tennis!" he said *triumphantly* as he *joyfully* tossed his racket into the air.

Intermediate: Here are the adverbs from the excerpt, with the words they modify:

Adverb	Modified word
aground	was driven (verb)
ashore	to get (verb)
badly	suffered (verb)
luckily	washed (verb)
ashore	washed (verb)
less	dramatic (adjective)
rarely	received (verb)
nearly	every (adjective)
simply	keeping (verb)

Advanced: This level calls on the student to fix a paragraph which is overloaded with overused adverbs. Notice how trite our paragraph is, and how the repeated *"-ly"* sound in the paragraph annoys the reader's ear. We ask the student to replace each italicized phrase with one word. In most cases the word will be an adjective or verb, but the student may come up with a vivid adverb.

Section C
Mind Quest

Some students will insist they have no ideas for writing and can't find any ideas. The four lessons in this section prod them to open their eyes and minds to the ideas all around them. A young writer interested in creative writing (such as fiction, plays and poetry) is probably already in tune with the constant search for ideas. Creative writers have lively imaginations and tend to live there, a habit which frustrates the people around them. *Any* writer of any specialty will benefit from staying on the prowl for ideas.

Lesson C1   Roaming Idea Hunt

Lesson Aims: To stimulate student's creative thinking; to practice active observation; to gather ideas even if the writer has no immediate use for them.

Watch for: Sharp observation; interest in ideas, especially a growing interest as the Idea Hunt progresses.

Start-Up: Beginning writers may need you to accompany them on the idea hunt. You can help them observe and suggest a few ideas to get started. Beginners should have a short time limit. Five minutes may be enough. You can always re-set the timer if the student wants to continue.

The student's notes can be about the simplest and most ordinary things. An unusual color on a leaf, a funny bug, an old book with several names written in the front, an unexplained sound from next door, the expression on a pet's face—those are all wonderful ideas to capture. Any could be the seed of a story or article. To notice small ordinary things may require more imagination than to see big unusual things.

Once the ideas are gathered, don't put pressure on a reluctant writer to turn them into stories. The purpose of this lesson is to practice *gathering* ideas. Let the beginning writer enjoy the idea hunt with no pressure to turn out a finished product at this point.

Intermediate and *Advanced*: Students who write a lot may have trouble isolating this part of the writing process as a separate exercise. The hunt will still be a helpful discipline and should yield some new ideas. We ask students to expand on their notes because these writers are ready to do something with the ideas they gather. Notice that the idea hunt for these students is internal as well as external.

All levels: Stress the importance of **saving notes in an idea file.** The next time the student insists there is nothing to write about, send him to his idea file. He will almost always find some gem he has forgotten. Any time the student remarks on something unusual, **suggest that he write it down and add it to his idea file.**

Lesson C2 Stationary Idea Hunt

Lesson Aims: To practice passive but alert observation; to practice gathering ideas even if the writer has no immediate use for them.

Watch for: Increasing awareness that ideas for writing are all around us.

This lesson is more of a challenge than Lesson C1 "Roaming Idea Hunt." In C1, the student gets to run around and actively search for ideas. We include this lesson because a writer needs the skill of patient observation even in unexciting circumstances.

Reasons for the three rules for the student's chosen spot: (1) The student is told to listen and needs something to hear; (2) TV and radio would feed ideas directly to the student and deaden his or her own observations; (3) when you sit down and "do nothing," food is always a distraction!

Start-Up: Beginning writers will have a large range of reactions to this lesson. On the first attempt, some will barely last one minute and won't find one thing to write down. Decide in advance if you will allow a bathroom break, because some students will beg for it. Others will get so carried away with ideas that they write right through their time limit.

The student's first attempt may look like a total flop: a lot of fidgeting and a blank piece of paper. **To sit still and simply observe might be a totally new experience for that student.** It's a big step to begin to catch on that interesting things happen when you sit still. So we give the student three tries. On the second attempt the student moves to a different spot, because maybe the first spot really was uninteresting. On the third attempt, the student goes back to the first spot in order to see it with fresh eyes. If he protests that there was nothing there the first time, encourage him to look and listen again for what he may have missed before. **You can give the student additional tries if you think the idea hunt is gaining momentum.**

Intermediate and *Advanced:* As with C1 "Roaming Idea Hunt," these students are ready to do something with the ideas they have gathered.

Option for all levels: Most students will do this lesson in a fairly quiet setting. An interesting option is to put the student in a busy crowded place such as a fair or a shopping mall. It's still a Stationary Idea Hunt because the student has to sit in one spot, but there is far more to see and hear. The stimulus of the busy public place is better than the TV or radio, because the TV or radio feeds messages (ideas) directly at the student, while in the public setting he observes others who probably ignore him.

Lesson C3   Create A Character

Lesson Aims: To understand basic features of characterization; to see the importance of knowing your characters well.

Watch for: Interest in characters and the possibilities of creating new characters.

This lesson uses the terms **character**, **obstacle** and **conflict**. Every child knows what those are, even if he doesn't know the words, because they are part of every story a child has ever heard, read, told or made up. All stories are in some way about a character who must solve a problem to reach a goal.

Start-Up: Read through the lesson instructions with your student. The explanatory material on page 28 may look like a lot of reading, but it isn't as complicated as it seems. Every child instinctively knows what a character is, and every child makes up imaginary characters long before he can write a story on paper. In an orderly way, the student now begins to create an original character.

Intermediate: Further questions help the student analyze the character and get to know him or her as well as possible. Note the importance of *knowing* the character thoroughly, so the writer does not have the character suddenly act in inconsistent ways.

Advanced: In addition to creating a character, the student begins to build a story based on the invented character.

Lesson C4   Create A Place

Lesson Aim: To explore the sense of place which the writer can create for the reader.

Watch for: Ability to imagine and describe details of a place.

This lesson uses the term **setting.** A story's setting is the place where the story happens. Settings are not limited to fiction. A true story has a setting which is a real place. Even in a true story, the writer has some choice of setting: will he tell about events which happened indoors or outdoors? in what parts of the indoors or outdoors?

Start-Up: Some students will be helped by drawing pictures of the imaginary place. The quality of the drawings does *not* matter so long as they help the writer picture the place. If the student has trouble getting started, ask some questions to help him think concretely:

> What color are the walls?
> What is the ceiling like?
> Is the floor hard or soft?
> Does it feel roomy here? cooped up? crowded?
> Can you see outside? If so, what do you see?
> Is the temperature comfortable, or is it too cold? too warm?
> Do you have fresh air?
> Is it noisy? quiet?
> What's the best thing about living here? What don't you like about it?

If the student breezes through one description and enjoys it, have him choose another setting and describe that. You can also let the student come up with other settings not on the list.

Intermediate: This activity calls for less imagination but more observation than *Start-Up*. The student must see a familiar place with fresh eyes and describe it for someone who has never seen it. You *and* your young writer will probably notice features you have never noticed about a familiar place.

Advanced: This level calls for some extended imagining of place. We provide questions to guide the student's imagination.

Section D
Lively Language

Good ideas deserve to be delivered in lively and interesting language. When language sparkles, it persuades. It pulls the reader over to the writer's side. Dull words make a writer's ideas sound like they aren't worth reading, no matter how good they are. These four lessons give young writers the tools to put sparkle and interest in their writing.

Lesson D1   Simile and the World Similes With You (Comparisons)

(The title of this lesson is a play on an old song title. If your student doesn't get it, that's okay.)

Lesson Aims: To identify two types of comparisons; to practice writing fresh comparisons.

Watch for: Some people naturally think in comparisons. Others struggle to compare one thing to another. Even if brilliant comparisons don't leap to your young writer's mind, they are a useful tool for any writer who will ever need to explain a complex idea.

This lesson introduces the terms **simile** and **metaphor.** Many people get them confused. In usage, the difference is obvious: the difference between "is like" (simile) and "is" (metaphor).

Start-Up: The introductory material of this lesson is long. We wanted to give a good explanation of similes and metaphors before we asked students to write any. You may want to read through the introduction with your writer. The student is asked to write down some familiar comparisons to spark his thinking. For a fun addition to this activity, ask friends and relatives for similes and metaphors they know. The student will probably have to define *simile* and *metaphor* for a few adults—a great opportunity to show off his new knowledge! After the stimulation of writing down "old standby" comparisons, the student invents new ones. Of course you don't have to stop at two metaphors and two similes.

Intermediate: The student must differentiate between simile and metaphor. Then the student is challenged to freshen up some overused similes and metaphors: the four we provide, and four more which he thinks of. Of course you don't have to stop at four additional ones.

Advanced: The parable of the prodigal son is a **metaphor** rather than a simile because it does not begin, "I will show you what God is *like* . . ." or "Repentance is *like.*" It begins, "There was a man who had two sons." Other parables of Jesus are similes; for example: "The kingdom of heaven is *like* a king who prepared a wedding banquet . . ." (Matthew 22:1).

Here is an interesting quote about similes. The writer Graham Greene noted in his journal: "Memories are a form of simile: when we say something is 'like' we are remembering."

Lesson D2 Megawatt Writing

Lesson Aim: To learn to turn up the intensity of our writing at definite points for definite reasons.

Watch for: Writing which genuinely grabs your attention at important points.

Start-Up: The questions will help the student shape a higher-intensity story. At this point the revised story is likely to be too busy and full of details. That's okay for now. When young writers are learning to add intensity, it is better to overdo the story than to leave it in the "blahs."

Intermediate: Advertising is designed to pound one idea into our heads, so it provides excellent practice in megawatt writing. When the student has rewritten the commercial, have him read it aloud (with expression!). Consider whether you would buy Whammo Laundry Soap based on this commercial. *You* can also read the commercial aloud and *ask the student* if he would buy Whammo Laundry Soap based on this commercial.

Advanced: The intensity of the student's writing should rise and fall. The student should demonstrate an ability to control the writing so it neither shouts all the time nor whispers all the time. The writer may find it easier to write the whole story at "high volume" and then tone down parts of it.

Lesson D3 Understatement

Lesson Aim: To see the value of restraint in writing.

Watch for: A feel of controlled restraint in the student's writing.

Start-Up: Younger students will need help to read through the instructions, not because of the concepts but because of the necessary use of big words: **exaggeration, opposite, understatement.** Fortunately every child knows what *exaggeration* is, even if the word itself is unfamiliar. *Opposite* is harder to explain but easy to demonstrate.

If your student does not quite get the idea of *understatement,* help him supply his own example. Ask: "Suppose you fall and really hurt your knee, but you don't want people to know how much it hurts. The next day somebody asks you, 'How's your knee?' What would you answer?" The student will probably answer "Not bad" or "It doesn't hurt much" or something similar. *That's understatement.* You hold back the strength of what you feel. (This approach is not perfect. The student might say "Fine." Keep trying!)

Intermediate: The writer may succeed in taking the edge off the exaggeration without bringing the paragraph all the way down to understatement. Don't be afraid to ask for a rewrite if the paragraph still does not feel restrained enough.

Advanced: As with the *Advanced* activity in Lesson D2, the writer may find it easier to write a piece in exaggerated style first and then bring it down to understated style. This could take two or more tries, each at lesser intensity.

A note on sarcasm: We don't get into it in this lesson, but *understatement is the heart of sarcasm.* If you turn your car too sharply and hit your garage, and your neighbor strolls over and remarks, "Maybe you should have come in a couple of inches to the left," that's sarcasm. It's also understatement. While nobody wants to encourage sarcasm in children, *it's a great tool for dialogue.* Put a few sarcastic remarks in the mouth of a character, and your reader has an excellent handle on that character. Sarcasm is a bitter sort of humor, and some writers will be tempted to overdo it. Sarcasm when overused is irritating and even boring.

Lesson D4   In Other Words

Lesson Aims: To learn to give attention to how experiences feel physically and emotionally; to practice describing an experience through its sensations.

Watch for: The final test of this sort of writing is made by the reader. If the writer is trying to communicate heat, does the reader feel the heat?

Start-Up: Some students may want to skip the questions and write the story. The student needs to first answer the questions—and any others you and the student think of—to analyze the details of the desert walk. The better the writer understands the experience, the more convincing the account will be.

Intermediate: The student explores the desert experience through the questions under *Start-Up*. More mature writers will assume these questions and ask them almost unconsciously, but they should still make notes of their answers. Their notes will show that they have gone through the questioning process. The act of writing down their answers will also make the imagined experience more concrete. Watch for the dual sensations of oppressive heat and fear in the student's writing.

Advanced: At this level the writer must dig into his own supply of memories and pull out a particular emotion. There is a chance the writer will get into the story and find it too uncomfortable. If you think this is happening, feel free to let the writer find a different topic.

All levels: If the finished work seems unconvincing, have the writer read it over again. Ask if the writer feels the heat (or other experience in *Advanced*). The writer may agree that it isn't quite there. Or he may insist that it *is* there because *he felt it when he wrote it.* The last answer is frustrating for both the writer and the reader. The reader doesn't get it, and the writer can't understand why the reader doesn't get it. If you come to a standoff, put the writing away for a few days, then let the student read it again. With fresh eyes, he may agree that it isn't quite there and be more open to discuss how to strengthen the work.

Section E
Special Features

The four lessons in this section focus on some specific elements which make a writer's work stronger and more convincing.

Lesson E1 Get A Grip: Titles

Lesson Aims: To see how an effective title gives the writer and the reader a good grip on the story; to generate title ideas; to start an ongoing title list.

Watch for: The place where the student stores the title list. Be sure it is easy to find later.

Start-Up: The introductory material is rather lengthy for a student who reads slowly. You may need to walk your student through it and help explain a few things along the way. The activity—starting a title list—is the easy part!

Intermediate and *Advanced:* Why not join the student and search for favorite titles in your own bookshelves and your own memory? Talk with the student about why you especially remember and like those titles.

Definition (optional): In the samples from my own title list, I mention that I like the repeated ch sound in "Last Chance for Cherries." A repeated beginning sound of words is called **alliteration.** If your student does not know the term, you can introduce it in the context of this lesson.

Lesson E2 Opening Hook

Lesson Aims: To realize the importance of a strong beginning; to practice recognizing and writing good opening hooks.

Watch for: Understanding that a good opening hook raises questions for the reader.

Note that we send students to look in books and magazines for good opening hooks. We do not send them to look in newspapers. The beginning of a news article is meant to *answer* questions, not raise them. The exception would be a feature article such as you find in the Travel or Health section of a newspaper.

The introductory material in this lesson uses the terms **fiction** and **non-fiction.** Some students may not be familiar with either term. Others will know "fiction" but not "non-fiction." You can explain that fiction is generally a made-up story, and non-fiction is anything else: a true story, a piece of opinion writing, history, even poetry.

Intermediate uses the terms **playwright** and **autobiography.** If the words are unfamiliar, have the student look them up. Or explain that a playwright is *someone who writes plays*, and an autobiography is *the story of a person's life, written by that person.* (Avoid a common spelling error: it's "playwright," not " playwrite"!)

Here is the actual first sentence of Moss Hart's *Act One:* "That afternoon, I went to work at the music store as usual." It's simple, but it raises the reader's curiosity with the phrase "as usual." The reader senses that something *un*usual is about to happen.

Lesson E3   Whose Point of View?

Lesson Aims: To identify various elements of point of view in storytelling; to practice the use of the most typical points of view.

Watch for: Note how readily the student picks up on the point of view of a published story or article. Some young writers will take to this lesson very naturally.

This lesson explains technical terms for points of view in writing: **first person, second person, third person; narrator,** (and under *Intermediate*) **omniscient** and **third person limited.**

Start-Up: If this level proves too abstract for beginning writers, don't worry too much about the technical terms. Find stories and articles written from different points of view and ask the student to look for differences in **who is telling the story.** In this case, examples will be the best teachers. Since second person is rare, the student will likely change from first person to third person, and from third person to first person.

Intermediate: At this level, students should learn the technical terms if they don't already know them. The rewrite activity will be especially interesting if the student takes a scene written from the point of view of the main character and writes it from the point of view of a very minor character, or the reverse: go from a minor character to the main character.

Advanced: If the student has done Lesson C3 "Create A Character," you can look back at what that lesson said about inanimate objects as characters (bottom of page 28).

Lesson E4   Let's Talk (Dialogue)

Lesson Aim: To help students write convincing dialogue by first listening to how people talk.

Watch for: Listening skills; awareness that different people will express the same ideas in different ways.

Good news! This lesson gives your young writer a reason to listen to you—and to other family members, friends and acquaintances.

This lesson concentrates on the written words of believable dialogue. It does not get into **attributives** (*he said, she said, So-and-So said*). In dialogue an unlimited number of verbs can stand in for *said: screamed, whimpered, stormed, yelled, assured, declared, exploded . . .* and on and on. In general it's best to stick with the simplest attributive: *said*. If the reader can easily keep track of who is speaking, the writer can skip the attributives and let the quotes stand alone. Introduce **attributives** as an additional feature of this lesson, if you feel the young writer will enjoy it and is ready for it.

Start-Up: In the introductory material, your student may have trouble with the words "individual" and "individually;" but there should be no problem understanding that people don't all talk exactly alike. If the student needs concrete help, have him tell you how different people he knows would explain something or describe something. Point out the contrasts.

Your biggest trouble with this activity may be that your young writer follows you and others too closely and listens too carefully! You may want to set limits of time and place for writing conversation. You may also want to warn other talkers in the area that their words are being recorded—on paper anyway.

As a fun challenge, after the student rewrites the quote, have him read both versions aloud to you. See if you can guess the speaker in each version.

Intermediate: This level stretches the demand on the student by asking for more rewritten quotes. Have the student read the original quotes and the rewrites aloud to you. See if you can guess the speaker in each version.

Advanced: In *Start-Up* and *Intermediate*, the student is asked to rewrite quotations as other, real people would say them. Here the student is asked to invent characters and rewrite the quotes to fit those characters. The student should not be expected to create fully-developed characters for this exercise, but he should get some idea of how each character would speak.

Section F
Even Better

When young writers are asked to revise their work, they often balk. (a) It sounds like too much effort. (b) It implies that what they wrote is not good enough. Both are probably true. Revising is like developing a skill in a sport or any other activity: we keep at it so we will improve. Revision discourages us less if we realize that a "first draft" is almost never a "FIRST draft." Much revision is automatic and unconscious. We think of several ways to word something before we write it down; and as we write, we cross out words and scribble in extra words. These four lessons help the writer make any piece of writing even better.

Lesson F1   The Minus Sign (Cutting)

Lesson Aims: To recognize what should be cut; to practice making cuts.

Watch for: Courage to eliminate words which get in the way of meaning; a sense of what advances the writer's purpose and what does not.

In the introductory material we advise the writer to "Remove anything which does not help you say what you want to say. Decide what matters, and cut what does not matter." Note that if the writer is not sure what he wants to say or doesn't know the purpose of the writing, he is **not ready to cut.** First the writer should get a **clear idea of his purpose in the work.**

Material which is cut does not have to go into the wastebasket. If the writer still likes the material, **save it!** Put it into that "deep freeze" idea file (see Lesson C1, bottom of page 25).

Start-Up and *Intermediate:* Have the student try to explain to you why he cut certain words.

Advanced: Every working writer has to cut good material just because it doesn't fit a certain space. It hurts. I went through this pain many times with the book you hold now, *Igniting Your Writing!* and with *The Jackpine Point Adventures*. Our printer produces books with pages in multiples of 8. We had decided that the *Jackpine Point* books would be 128 pages long, and I did not want useless blank pages at the beginning or end of the books. One extra page of text from me would jump the book from 128 pages to 136 pages: one page of text and seven blanks!

With *Igniting Your Writing!* we wanted each lesson to fit on two pages, beginning on the left side, so the entire lesson lies open in front of the student. Too much material would necessitate a new page, and the next lesson would begin on the right. We could have started new lessons halfway down a page, but that seemed clumsy and confusing.

As writers, we would like to think we can write whatever we want. Once we start to work professionally with editors and printers, we are constrained by certain boundaries. Some of those limits are negotiable. Most are beyond the writer's control. I could write lots more on this subject, but as you can see, I'm out of room.

Lesson F2   The Plus Sign (Expanding)

Lesson Aims: To identify unanswered questions in a piece of writing; to fill in the gaps with necessary information.

Watch for: Willingness to see the writing from the reader's point of view; awareness of places in the writing where the reader needs to know more.

In Lesson F1 we talked about the pain of cutting our work. As much as it hurts to cut, I think it is easier to cut than to expand. When we cut, at least we work with existing material. When we expand, we must research or invent material to fill in gaps.

Expanding is not padding! We all know about padding a research paper with verbose opinions and hot air in order to stretch four pages to the required ten pages. **Expanding means filling in communication gaps, not filling space.** If you feel your student is starting to pad rather than communicate, go back and explore the questions of "Who? What? Where? When? Why? How?" from page 50.

Start-Up: Just about any details your young writer invents will be fine, as long as they reasonably fit the basic idea of the original sentence. Here is an example of rewritten sentences #1 and #4:

> Here comes our new neighbor, that skinny guy with the old push lawn mower, wanting to mow our lawn again just because we helped him move in.

> Oh no, we're going to be stuck in this airport another night because it looks like it's going to snow a lot!

Intermediate: The possibilities for an expanded rewrite are as wide as your student's imagination. Watch that the writer does not simply stretch out the paragraph with strings of adjectives. ("Candace was sorry she had ever thought of going back down into the *dark, damp, spooky, smelly* basement. The *big, old, battered, mysterious, wooden* box was open now.") That's okay in a first draft to help collect ideas, but the writer should be able to move on and find more valuable information which genuinely helps the reader.

Advanced: Have the writer first study the *Intermediate* paragraph as an example of a story with insufficient information. *Intermediate* does three things: it stretches the student's ability to see when a piece of writing is insufficient (because he has to write an insufficient piece), it calls for imagination as he fills in gaps, and it demonstrates his ability to repair his own work—something a working writer has to do all the time.

Lesson F3   I Can Fix That For You

Lesson Aim: To rewrite someone else's work based on what the student has learned and practiced throughout this course.

Watch for: Increased proficiency in many of the skills presented throughout this book. You should not expect your student to demonstrate mastery of all areas in the one rewrite assigned in this lesson. Look for **any areas of improvement.**

This lesson and Lesson F4 will help the student apply, in concentrated form, the skills taught throughout *Igniting Your Writing!* Take on this lesson and Lesson F4 only if your student has **completed all or most of the lessons (at appropriate level) in Sections A, B, D, and E.** (Section C "Mind Quest" is less applicable to revision.)

This lesson lacks the familiar *Start-Up, Intermediate,* and *Advanced* headings. The lesson level will be determined by the level of difficulty of the piece the student takes on to rewrite.

Don't hesitate to supervise your student's choice of a work to rewrite. It should be of a length and difficulty which you think appropriate for the student's skill.

A poorly-written letter to the editor is fertile ground for a rewrite, especially if the subject is interesting. Almost any skill the student applies will improve the letter. Tackling a rewrite of an excellent work may give your student the false idea that he can do better. But who knows? Maybe he can!

This assignment will take your student longer than any of the other lessons in this book (except Lesson F4). **Be sure the student takes breaks.** If you do not ordinarily talk through assignments with your student, offer to talk through this one. **Stretch out this lesson over several days if necessary.**

If the chosen piece proves overwhelming, help your student select another one—but only after the student has made an honest try. **You may choose to leave a long piece half-revised,** if the student struggles through and does well in the first half but then gets burnt out. He has still accomplished a tough bit of rewriting.

Although this lesson and Lesson F4 were not written as tests, **you can choose to use either or both as a final exam for this course.**

Your student can **continue to rewrite published pieces for practice,** using the summing-up questions in this lesson. Push up the degree of difficulty simply by picking longer and more compex pieces to revise.

Lesson F4 Nobody's Perfect

Lesson Aim: To rewrite a piece of the student's own writing, based on what the student has learned and practiced throughout this course.

Watch for: Increased proficiency in many of the skills presented throughout this book. As with Lesson F3, don't expect your student to demonstrate mastery of all areas in the one rewrite assigned in this lesson. **Look for any areas of improvement.**

This is a payoff lesson for you and your student. Like Lesson F3, it will help the student apply, in concentrated form, the skills taught throughout *Igniting Your Writing!* Now the student ties it all together to see how much better the writing can be.

Take on this lesson only if your student has **completed all or most of the lessons (at appropriate level) in Sections A, B, D, and E.** (Section C "Mind Quest" is less applicable to revision.)

Like Lesson F3, this lesson lacks *Start-Up, Intermediate,* and *Advanced* headings. It doesn't matter how you label the effort; when a writer takes on a rewrite of his own work, it always *feels* like *Advanced!*

This lesson is the reason (among other reasons) that we told you to keep your student's writings throughout this course. Your student now has **a body of work from which to choose a piece for revision.** Even if the student has done everything at *Start-Up* level, you should have a good collection of sentences. You—or you and your student together—can pick out some sentences for rewrites.

Although this lesson and Lesson F3 were not written as tests, **you can choose to use either or both as a final exam for this course.**

Your student should continue to rewrite his own work, using the summing-up questions in this lesson. As the title says, "Nobody's Perfect" and no one turns out flawless work on the first try.

Rewriting is the constant work of the serious writer. So to all young writers, and to their chief cheerleaders, their parents/teachers as well . . .

Keep writing!

Problems Chart

Make notes of mistakes or problems in the student's work. As this chart grows, it will begin to show which problems are only **occasional** and which are **chronic**. You can then work on the persistent flaws in separate practices. *Photocopy this sheet as many times as needed.*

Lesson #	Grammar	Spelling	Punctuation	Organization (including paragraphs)	More Variety	More Imaginative Language	Other

Strengths Chart

Use this chart to keep a record of particularly strong points of the student's writing. Over time, this chart will reveal **consistent** strengths which can show a student's emerging talent for a particular type of writing. Let the student see or hear this list as you add new entries. *Photocopy this sheet as many times as needed.*

Here are some possible strong points of a piece of writing:

clarity	realism	colorful description	reads smoothly
humor	good dialogue	well organized	rhythm of the words
perfect or improved grammar	venture into new type of writing	variety—not boring	emotion
perfect or improved spelling	imaginative	concise and to-the-point	sound of the words

Sometimes it is hard to pin down the reason a particular piece of writing is strong. You only know it moved you deeply. That may be the strongest point of all, but the hardest to explain on a chart.

Lesson #_____   This was particularly good:

Sources of Quotations

Jerry Adler, "Shooting To The End," *Newsweek,* Oct. 15, 2001, p. 70.

Webb Chiles, *The Open Boat Across the Pacific,* W.W. Norton & Company, NY, 1982, p. 26.

Charles Dickens, *A Christmas Carol,* Classics Club edition, Walter J. Black, NY, 1932, p. 1.

Julio de la Torre, *Owls: Their Life and Behavior,* Crown Publishers, Inc., NY, 1990, p. viii.

Arthur Conan Doyle, "The Adventure of the Speckled Band," from *The Original Illustrated Sherlock Holmes,* Castle, Secaucus, NJ, n.d., p. 108.

Graham Greene, *In Search of a Character: Two African Journals,* Viking Press, NY, 1962, pp. 10, 31.

Moss Hart, *Act One: An Autobiography,* Random House, NY, 1959, p. 3.

Marguerite Henry, *Brighty of the Grand Canyon,* Rand McNally & Co., Chicago, 1953, p. 132.

Thor Heyerdahl, *Kon-Tiki,* tr. F.H. Lyon, Doubleday, NY, 1950, Permabooks edition, p. 9.

Charles K. Hyde, *The Northern Lights: Lighthouses of the Upper Great Lakes,* Wayne State University Press, Detroit, MI, 1995, p. 69.

John Knowles, *A Separate Peace,* The Macmillan Co., NY, 1959, p. 93.

Sandy Larsen, *The Re-Appearing Statue, Ice Festival, Something's Fishy, The Dark Lighthouse,* Merritt Park Press, Greenville, IL, various pages.

Jack London, "To Build A Fire," from *The Collected Jack London,* Steven J. Kaspin, ed., Barnes & Noble, NY, 1992, p. 8.

Edgar Allan Poe, "The Tell-tale Heart," from *Complete Stories of Edgar Allan Poe,* International Collectors Library, NY, 1966, p. 121.

Chaim Potok, *The Chosen,* Fawcett Publications, Greenwich, CT, 1967, p.9.

Kathleen Ritmeyer, "The Rebirth of the British Museum," *Biblical Archaeology Review,* Sept./Oct. 2001, p. 52.

"Saki" (H.H. Munro), "Reginald," from *The Short Stories of Saki,* Modern Library edition, NY, 1951, p.3.

Pamela Selbert, "Olney Residents Take Pleasure In Their Little White Treasures," *St. Louis Post-Dispatch,* Nov. 4, 2001, p. T10.

John Steinbeck, *Travels With Charley in Search of America,* Viking Press, NY, 1961, p. 154.

William Strunk Jr. and E.B. White, *The Elements of Style,* third ed., Macmillan Publishing Co., Inc., NY, 1979, p. 21.

James Thurber, "The Topaz Cufflinks Mystery," from *The Thurber Carnival,* Harper & Brothers, NY, 1945, p. 119.

E.B. White, *Charlotte's Web,* Harper & Brothers, NY, 1952, p. 1.

E.B. White, *Stuart Little,* Harper & Brothers, NY, 1945, p. 1.

P.G. Wodehouse, *The Code of the Woosters,* Vintage Books, Random House, NY, 1975 (orig. 1938), p. 102.

Meet the Author

Sandy Larsen has been a professional freelance writer since 1981. She is the author of the *Jackpine Point Adventure* fiction series for older elementary/junior high readers.

With her husband Dale Larsen she has co-authored over fifty books and Bible study guides for major Christian publishers such as InterVarsity Press, Harold Shaw Publishers and Scripture Press.

Sandy has led writing workshops for homeschool groups, Christian schools and bookstores in Minnesota, Wisconsin, Michigan and Illinois. She especially enjoys the lively question-and-answer times with young writers. She has about 15 years' experience teaching junior high Sunday school and has served as both a junior high and high school youth leader.

Dale and Sandy taught English in Ukraine as volunteers with Educational Services International. During that year they had to produce almost all their own curriculum with very limited resources.

Sandy is a graduate of Greenville College, Greenville, Illinois. She enjoys hiking in the woods, canoeing, camping, all aspects of community theatre and—of course—reading. After twenty years on Lake Superior, she and Dale recently moved to Greenville to the house where Sandy grew up. She has started to read her way through the hundreds of books which were in the house, a task (no, a joy) she expects to take many years.

Are you ready for a Jackpine Point Adventure?

Loaded with laughs, action, mystery and surprises, *The Jackpine Point Adventures* tell the story of five young friends, two girls and three boys, who live up north on the shore of the Big Lake. Narrator David Malloy meets an unpredictable array of problems in cheerful—though occasionally confused—style. Along the way he must decide what to do about friendships, loyalty and faith. As their Sunday school teacher says, "Wherever the Jackpine Pointers are, something is bound to *occur.*"

Each *Jackpine Point Adventure* has an online study guide to help you teach writing skills and discuss the values in the books.

#1 *The Re-Appearing Statue*   ISBN 0-9666677-0-0
#2 *Ice Festival*   ISBN 0-9666677-1-9
#3 *Something's Fishy*   ISBN 0-9666677-2-7
#4 *The Dark Lighthouse*   ISBN 0-9666677-3-5

**Merritt Park Press
910 N. Elm St.
Greenville, IL 62246
618-664-2207
dslarsen@merrittpark.com**

www.merrittpark.com

Permissions Statement

Contents © Sandy Larsen 2002

Except as stated, no part of this book may be reproduced in any form without written permission from Merritt Park Press.

Merritt Park Press
910 N. Elm St.
Greenville, IL 62246
618-664-2207
dslarsen@merrittpark.com

www.homeschoolwriting.com